HEIDEGGER AND THE MEDIA

Theory and the Media

HEIDEGGER AND THE MEDIA

DAVID J. GUNKEL AND
PAUL A. TAYLOR

polity

First published in 2014 by Polity Press

65 Bridge Street
Cambridge CB2 1UR, UK

Polity Press
350 Main Street
Malden, MA 02148, USA

ISBN-13: 978-0-7456-6125-4
ISBN-13: 978-0-7456-6126-1(pb)

A catalogue record for this book is available from the British Library.

Typeset in 10.75 on 14 pt Janson Text
by Servis Filmsetting Ltd, Stockport, Cheshire
Printed and bound in Great Britain by Clays Ltd, St Ives plc

For further information on Polity, visit our website: www.politybooks.com

CONTENTS

PREFACE

> I am a philosopher, not a scientist, and we philosophers are
> better at questions than answers. I haven't begun by insult-
> ing myself and my discipline, in spite of first appearances.
> Finding better questions to ask, and breaking old habits
> and traditions of asking, is a very difficult part of the grand
> human project of understanding ourselves and our world.
>
> Dennett 1996: vii

Philosophy, unlike the empirical sciences or other inves-
tigative activities, is not necessarily concerned with
answers. Like the American philosopher Daniel Dennett,
Heidegger is not interested in providing solutions to existing questions and debates but is dedicated to re-examining
all those questions that have typically been asked in a
relatively uncritical fashion. Heidegger highlights the
predominantly unacknowledged ways in which the very
typicality of our conventional modes of inquiry already
over-determine what can be asked about, what evidence

will count as appropriate and what outcomes might be possible.

We do not deny that this makes reading Heidegger challenging, if not frustrating, in a manner for which the contemporary reader may be ill prepared. We live in an age in which questions generally demand immediate answers, and it is often considered bad form to respond to a question with another question. But this is precisely what Heidegger does and, in our view, this is what represents authentic philosophical endeavour – a much-needed form of inquiry that has increasingly been siphoned off by self-styled 'social sciences' in which the fetishization of methodology frequently acts as a poor alibi for genuine thought.

In keeping with this philosophical commitment to critical inquiry, however, a question immediately arises concerning Heidegger and his infamous entanglement with Nazism. According to Miguel de Beistegui (2005: 155), 'no aspect of Heidegger's life and work is more controversial than his engagement in favour of National Socialism, and his tenure as the first Nazi rector of the University of Freiburg from May 1933 to April 1934.' Although Heidegger only occupied the position of rector for twelve months, he remained a member of the party through the end of the war and was officially classified a Nazi *Mitläufer*, or 'fellow traveller', in March 1949 by the State Commission for Political Purification as part of the post-war de-Nazification process. Heidegger presented his own account of this difficult period in an interview with the German magazine *Der Spiegel* published posthumously in 1976 (a precondition for his agreement to talk). Despite his rationale, most scholars find Heidegger's public explanations to be woefully inadequate and persistently unapologetic – leading to more questions than answers. And one of those questions that still needs to be addressed is what, if anything, can or should be salvaged from Heidegger's work?

Our belief that Heidegger's thinking still justifies persevering with rests upon two central points:

1 Refusing to engage with Heidegger's philosophy achieves little because of the profound influence he had upon a range of distinctly non-Nazi and vehemently anti-fascist thinkers such as Hannah Arendt, Herbert Marcuse, Jean-Paul Sartre and Jacques Derrida. A proper understanding of these and other historically important thinkers necessitates engagement with Heidegger's writing *whatever censure we may wish to impose upon the man himself.*

2 There is nothing in Heidegger's philosophy that is innately fascistic. In fact, his critique of technology explored in this book raises profound issues about technology's role in dehumanizing people, of which the Nazi death camps were the darkest historical manifestation. In this case, unalloyed censure of Heidegger's thought based upon his deeply flawed political affiliation is not only an inadequate response – it misses an opportunity to understand better the role technology played in facilitating Nazi ideology.

The first justification falls outside the remit of a book about media technology, but the second relates to Heidegger's unique perspective concerning the concept of *essence* as it relates to our contemporary mediated environment, where (foreshadowing Marshall McLuhan's famous adage 'The medium is the message') we often miss the fundamental social effects of media due to our tendency to be distracted by the relatively superficial significance of their content when compared to their form.

In fact, this concern is clearly evident in one of the very passages relating to the Holocaust that Heidegger's critics put forward as proof that he should be viewed as an intellectual *persona non grata*. In a 1949 lecture entitled *Das Gestell*

(Enframing), Heidegger described how 'agriculture is now a mechanized food industry, in essence the same as the production of corpses in the gas chambers and extermination camps, the same thing as the blockading and starving of countries, the same thing as the production of hydrogen bombs' (BFL: 27). The equivalences Heidegger asserts here led to such representative criticisms as Davidson's (1989: 424) observation that 'when one encounters Heidegger's 1949 pronouncement, one cannot but be staggered by his inability – call it metaphysical inability – to acknowledge the everyday fate of bodies and souls, as if the bureaucratized burning of selected human beings were not all that different from the threat to humanity posed in the organization of the food industry by the forces of technology.' Using the phrase 'were not all that different', Davidson fundamentally misses Heidegger's central philosophical point. By concentrating solely on the expression 'the same thing as', Davidson thereby ignores the crucial qualification contained in the immediately preceding phrase 'in essence'. It is with this particular concept that Heidegger's work, despite, we repeat, the eminently understandable reservations one might have about the man himself, provides profoundly important insights into the social impact of technology, and, in particular, media technology.

It is critically important to note here that Heidegger is *not* saying that the mechanization of agriculture and the extermination camps are equivalent phenomena. Instead, the similarity being alluded to is one of *essence*, and it is this conceptualization that has profound implications for our understanding of media as an integral part of a diverse technological environment that shares certain *essential* features. As Heidegger aptly described it, 'the same is never the equivalent [*das Gleiche*]. The same is just as little a merely undifferentiated confluence of the identical. The same is much more the relation of differentiation' (BFL: 49). Apparently self-contradictory, both this statement and the subsequent utterance that 'the essence of technology is by no means anything technological' (QCT: 4) highlight the fact that, whilst there are many different forms of technological artefact, common across such diverse forms is an underlying similarity, namely the facilitation of an objectifying attitude towards existence. This is an important insight into the essence of technology that informs much of the subsequent chapters' specific attention to media and the process of mediation.

Thus, along with Heidegger, prominent Jewish thinkers like Zygmunt Bauman and Richard Bernstein also insist upon the wider and more generalizable significance of the uniquely industrial nature of the Holocaust. For example, in terms that directly resonate with Heidegger's language, Bauman argues:

> Like everything else in our modern society, the Holocaust was an accomplishment in every respect superior if measured by the standards that this society has preached and institutionalized. It towers high above the past genocidal episodes in the same way as the modern industrial plant towers above the craftsman's cottage workshop, or the modern industrial farm with its tractors, combines and pesticides, towers above the peasant farmstead with its horse, hoe and hand-weeding. (Bauman 1989: 89)

Similarly, Bernstein pointed out how 'we may find it almost impossible to imagine how someone could "think" (or rather, not think) in this manner, whereby manufacturing food, bombs, or corpses are "in essence the same" and where this can become "normal," "ordinary" behavior. This is the mentality that [Hannah] Arendt believed she was

facing in Eichmann' (Bernstein 1996: 170). The mistake
we often make is to think that such a mentality is limited to
such exceptional figures as Eichmann. The truly disturbing
point of Arendt's *Eichmann in Jerusalem* is contained within
its resonant subtitle – *A Report on the Banality of Evil*. Any
evil proclivities present in Eichmann were vastly overshad-
owed by the harm he caused as an otherwise unremarkable
bespectacled functionary in a huge technological system
devoted to the dehumanization of a whole people. The fact
of Heidegger's questionable past therefore does not, on its
own, do away with the need to confront the stubbornly persistent implications of his ontological analysis of the essence
of technology for our own historical predicament.

Hence, notwithstanding the myriad reasons for scepticism
of the man himself, we remain drawn to Heidegger's work
because it epitomizes the fact that 'the task of philosophy is
not to provide answers or solutions, but to submit to critical
analysis the questions themselves, to make us see how the
very way we perceive a problem is an obstacle to its solution'
(Žižek 2006a: 137). This book, therefore, *does not* aim to
provide readers with a neat ('ready-to-hand' in Heidegger's
terminology) framework with which to update Heidegger's
key ideas unproblematically for today's mediascape. This
would involve a performative contradiction – an instrumen-
talized critique of instrumentalism; a theoretical tool that
paradoxically seeks to question fundamentally the nature of
tools. Our much more modest aim is to encourage readers
to question more forcefully both conventional approaches
to the media and the conventional media representations of
Heidegger. This objective, whatever its limitations, at least
remains true to a key Heideggerian aphorism to which we
wholeheartedly subscribe and return to throughout this book
– 'questioning is the piety of thought' (QCT: 35).

ACKNOWLEDGEMENTS

This book was, we told ourselves, supposed to be easy to write. Paul had just finished writing *Žižek and the Media* (2010) and was therefore familiar with the format and tone necessary for the series. David had just completed *The Machine Question: Critical Perspectives on AI, Robots and Ethics* (2012), which, among other things, developed a method for using the work of Martin Heidegger to investigate recent innovations in information and communication technology.

We were wrong. This book turned out to be more difficult than we anticipated, but for good reason. In fact, as we began to develop the chapters, everything we thought we already knew about media and about Heidegger became questionable and question-worthy. Not that we are complaining. This is exactly what we had hoped to present in the book – a deliberate and explicit challenge to rethink both the work of Martin Heidegger and what we ordinarily call 'the media' – we just did not know how far down this would go.

In the process of traversing this path (to use a distinctly

Heideggerian metaphor), we have been assisted by a number of others whom we wish to recognize by name. Thanks from both of us to Andrew J. Mitchell for providing early access to his translation of the Bremen and Freiburg lectures.

For Paul, a big shout out to the Victoria pub 'Booth Group' – David, Ben, Melissa, Stuart, Heidi, Calvin and Sita – and lots of love and thanks to Rachel, and Barbie the bull terrier, for the 'good life' at the Cymraeg version of Heidegger's Black Forest retreat, Wyau Hapus!

For David, a *danke sehr* to those individuals who showed the way to reading Heidegger: Thomas Sheehan, John Sallis and David Farrell Krell; and a *dziękuje bardzo i dużo miłości* to Anja, Stas and Maki.

INTRODUCTION

Guns don't kill people. People kill people.
  Unofficial slogan of the National Rifle Association

The essence of technology is by no means anything technological.

QCT: 4

In the absence of precise statistics, we strongly suspect that
the majority of self-styled liberal academics would vehemently disagree with the above NRA-associated sentiment.
This is because those in favour of gun control (or at least some
level of regulation) tend to readily embrace the seemingly
logical notion that guns play a technologically determining
role in violence. The presence of military assault rifles in
urban settings, for example, is likely to lead to more fatali-
ties compared to the presence of non-automatic weapons or
no guns at all. Interestingly, however, amongst similar academics in the fields of Media and Communications Studies

one frequently encounters a largely unquestioned belief in the essential neutrality of technology. This belief repeatedly manifests itself in variations on the basic mantra: 'it's not the technology you use, but how you choose to use it that is important' – a view that Langdon Winner (1977: 27) termed the 'myth of neutrality' and dismissed as 'a truism striving to be a bromide'. Despite being seldom acknowledged by media scholars (or if acknowledged, only cursorily), Heidegger's philosophical approach to technology raises a profound challenge to those who selectively endorse and critique technological determinism, an issue that, with the advent of ubiquitous computing (*ubicomp*) and such new forms of subtly unobtrusive technological mediation as Google's new *Glass* interface, has never been more pertinent.

Although seemingly paradoxical, Heidegger's pronouncement that the essence of technology lies beyond the particular characteristics of any specific technological contrivance encapsulates the manner in which his work encourages us to consider the determining qualities of technological *environments* rather than individual artefacts. The homespun saying 'when you have a hammer, everything looks like a nail' expresses this determinist quality, this alteration in our mindset that occurs when we start using a simple tool. The change introduced when the artefact at hand is a complex piece of technology is exponentially greater, and then greater still when considering the use of technologies that rely upon an integrated system of mutually referential technologies such as the digital matrices that surround us today. What makes Heidegger uniquely important for the study of media technology is the manner in which his seemingly unfashionable notion of technology helps us to reflect upon the general nature of the technocratic mindset. We argue that this is ultimately much more significant than the specific peculiarities of individual artefacts whether they be hammers, iPads or the internet.

THE ONTOLOGY OF *DASEIN*

Dasein is an entity which does not just occur among other entities. Rather it is ontically distinguished by the fact that, in its very Being, that Being is an *issue* for it. But in that case, this is a constitutive state of Dasein's Being, and this implies that Dasein, in its Being, has a relationship towards that Being – a relationship which itself is one of Being. And this means further that there is some way in which Dasein understands itself in its Being, and that to some degree it does so explicitly. It is peculiar to this entity that with and through its Being, this Being is disclosed to it. *Understanding of Being is itself a definite characteristic of Dasein's Being.* Dasein is ontically distinctive in that it *is* ontological.

BT: 32

Since it is the use of untranslated terms like *Dasein* that is a likely contributor to Heidegger's reputation for incomprehensibility, it is worth tackling this term's significance straight away. In standard German, the word *Dasein* means 'existence'. Heidegger, however, uses the word in its more literal sense of 'there being' as an expression of the kind of being that is characteristic of human existence. Obviously, German was the language of Heidegger's original texts, but the fact that the term remains untranslated in standard translations of his writings is an indication of the special work it is designed to carry out. *Dasein* conveys something about the unique nature of *being human* that is not adequately articulated by the available vocabulary, like 'human nature', 'human being' or 'human existence'. A key feature of the term that we will repeatedly return to throughout this book is its positionality, its being-in-the-world – something that is, for better or worse, not expressible with a single English word (or any other word in any other language, for that matter). Additionally, Heidegger's use of the term *Dasein* immediately introduces us to the significance of the philosophical distinction between the ontic and the ontological. The ontic indicates that which exists, whilst ontological refers to the being of beings, or how the existence of those things is supported or structured. Much more than just an esoteric philosophical distinction, recognizing the difference between the ontic and the ontological is particularly important for understanding the nature of mediated Being.

For Heidegger, *Dasein* only makes sense in terms of a particular comportment towards Being. Being, however, is not, as Heidegger points out, able to be experienced as such; it does not exist alongside and come to be encountered as just another entity. For this reason, Being is that which we most take for granted and routinely fail to reflect upon. For example, we are so familiar with the conjoined (and upon reflection partially redundant) term *human beings*, that we tend to assume automatically the natural relationship between the two words rather than recognize the precise way in which *together* they express the inseparability of what we understand as 'human' and 'being'. The curious obtrusiveness of the word *Dasein* (an obtrusiveness that is also evident in the German text and not just in translation) is deliberately used by Heidegger to call attention to this problem and cause us to think reflectively about something that often goes by without a second thought. Although the above quotation from Heidegger might initially appear more confusing than helpful, given the complexity of what Heidegger is trying to articulate about *Dasein*, it actually constitutes a direct statement of the term's centrality to his insistently ontological approach. Namely, that an 'understanding of Being is itself a definite characteristic of *Dasein*'s Being'. In other words, *Dasein* is not just one entity existing among other entities. What distinguishes *Dasein* is that it is the one entity that in

its very being is concerned with *Being*. Or as Heidegger succinctly summarizes it, '*Dasein* is ontically distinctive in that
it is ontological.'

But what does all this philosophizing possibly have to do
with media? Our answer is that *Dasein* – both the obtrusive
materiality of the word itself and the ontological concept
to which it refers – raises a series of fundamental questions
about the nature of *being mediated* and *mediated being* that
have been largely ignored by media scholars due to, at best,
indifferent neglect and, at worst, intellectually defensive
and short-sighted claims that Heidegger is obscurantist and
muddle-headed. Rejecting this characterization outright, we
propose that Heidegger's ontology enables us to understand
the fundamental basis, the *primum mobile*, of the act of mediation. This understanding then sheds light on its subsequent
embodiment in a whole range of media manifestations that
culminate in today's 'ubicomp' environment. Each with their
own particular focus, the following four chapters all examine different aspects of Heidegger's thought to show how
we live in a mediated environment in which the distinction
between being and Being or the ontic and the ontological
has become increasingly indistinguishable. Although we risk
being accused of taking the reader away from a direct focus
upon media technology, this book takes Heidegger at his
word when he says that 'the essence of technology is by no
means anything technological'. We therefore unapologetically focus on the essential aspects of media that, somewhat
paradoxically, are better understood when one moves away
from specific media examples and instead concentrates upon
the broader implications for a society pervaded by mediated objects and techniques of objectification. In this way,
Heidegger's thought provides access to a core aspect of
mediated life that more overtly media-focused approaches
are actually ill-equipped to consider.

CHAPTER SUMMARIES

1 We Need to Talk About Media

The first chapter deals with the originating act of mediation, that is, language. It explores Heidegger's innovative thesis that we not only speak language, but language also speaks us – a formulation that paved the way for subsequent explorations of this theme by influential post-structuralist thinkers like Jacques Lacan, Julia Kristeva, Jean Baudrillard and Jacques Derrida. Following the twists and turns of Heidegger's life-long engagement with this subject, the chapter analyses two common theories of language – the instrumental and constitutive views. This analysis of what is considered to be an essential form of mediation provides the crucial groundwork for understanding the rest of this book's focus on the underlying processes at work in media – the seemingly obvious but often under-appreciated effort to *mediate* all things.

2 Mediated Truth

Building on chapter 1's account of the manner by which media do not just represent things but also construct the world they portray, chapter 2 examines the way in which, with misleading equanimity, western culture has come to equate the concept of truth with correctness of representation. In other words, the second chapter is concerned with the standard account of the process of mediation, whereby media represent real things in the world and that the truth of what is represented can be assessed by measuring how well the mediated representations correspond to and correctly portray the facts on the ground. This traditional and long-standing formulation is contrasted with Heidegger's stubborn insistence on the conceptual distinction to be made between what is true and what is merely correct. This rather heady philosophical point is then practically illustrated by using the notion of *communicatively determinative exhibition* to demonstrate how contemporary media society is the culmination of a historic development in western thought that increasingly privileges correctness as truth, and the chapter explores the consequences of this taken-for-granted and culturally ingrained bias.

3 In Medias Res

The third chapter considers the position of media as always already 'in the middle of things'. Here Heidegger's concepts of the *ready-to-hand* and *present-to-hand* are described in detail in order to help explain the essential difference that exists in his work between *things*, *objects* and *equipment*. Media technologies are shown to occupy a unique position in this schema due to the manner in which they straddle the distinction between inanimate objects (media hardware) and representations (software and media content). We see how, for Heidegger, it is a mistake to approach individual pieces of technology in isolation from the overarching equipmental totality to which they simultaneously contribute and derive their own form of being.

4 The Design of Media Apps: The Questions Concerning Technology

The final chapter brings together the previously encountered themes of mediation, representation and positionality to demonstrate how, despite accusations of being anachronistically nostalgic and folksy, or *völkisch*, Heidegger's philosophy still has much to say about cutting-edge media innovations. In keeping with Heidegger's use of deliberately obtrusive

neologisms, we use the term *Dasign* to question the implications for *Dasein* of the historically unprecedented media
saturation of contemporary life. Heidegger's comments
upon the modern media's creation of uniform *distancelessness* is shown to have direct (but seldom commented-upon)
relevance to the work of a wide range of theorists including
such ostensibly unlikely candidates as Theodor Adorno and
Jean Baudrillard.

THEMATIC SUMMARY

Taken together, the book's main themes of *language*, *truth*,
telepresence and *technological determinism* constitute the four
key, related aspects of what makes Heidegger's purportedly
abstract and esoteric work so useful for revealing very practical and radical insights into the media's role as a structuring
element of our everyday lives.

1 Heidegger's language

> Rorty predicted that philosophers 'for centuries to come'
> will benefit from Heidegger's 'original and powerful nar-
> rative' of the history of philosophy from the Greeks to
> Nietszche. I doubt this very much . . . Heidegger will con-
> tinue to fascinate those hungry for mysticism of the anaemic
> and purely verbal variety, the 'glossogonous metaphysics' of
> which his philosophy is such an outstanding example . . .
> More sober and rational persons will continue to regard the
> whole Heidegger phenomenon as a grotesque aberration of
> the human mind.
>
> Edwards 2004: 47

Given our claims concerning the importance of Heidegger's
analysis of technology, one question that immediately arises

is why his work has not had wide acceptance and attention within Media and Communication Studies? Beyond the question of his involvement with National Socialism, one reason can be found in Heidegger's unique mode of expression that has led 'most philosophers in the Anglo-American tradition' to dismiss him as 'an obscurantist muddlehead' (Searle 2000: 71). Negative reactions like this and the above obloquy from Paul Edwards have succeeded in creating a reputation for Heidegger's incomprehensibility that draws upon his undeniable use of numerous neologisms, preposition-dependent German phrases, and pseudo-mystical conceptions (i.e. the *Saving Power* and the *Four-Fold*). These different linguistic manoeuvres perhaps account for why readers tend to approach Heidegger with either initial suspicion before they have read any of his work or a growing sense of frustration once they have, but we believe that there is substantially more to it than this.

First of all, and most practically, responses such as those of Edwards and others, fail to solve the innate problem encountered when attempting genuinely original philosophical investigation with a common-sense mode of expression. Although it is assumed to be the *sine qua non* of successful communication, intelligibility is not necessarily what we conventionally assume it to be. So that 'in his *Beiträge zur Philosophie (Vom Ereignis)*, Heidegger claims: "making itself intelligible is the suicide of philosophy." He defines intelligibility in terms of the modern metaphysical forms of thinking and speaking about beings as objects of representation. Moreover, intelligibility involves a uniform accessibility for the inauthentic anybody of an age marked by thoughtlessness' (Gregory 2007: 57). Crucial for the purposes of this book is the phrase 'speaking about beings as objects of representation'. This touches directly on the interrelationship in Heidegger's work between things and

the various under-acknowledged ways in which we routinely transform things into *objects*. Gender politics is one
of the few areas where the ideological implications of this
process of objectification are commonly recognized. Much
more common is the way we typically fail to recognize
the widespread operation of various processes of objectification in which the media play a particularly pivotal
role.

Heidegger's work jolts us from accepting what otherwise
'goes without saying' in a radical manner. As William Lovitt
(QCT: xvi) argues, Heidegger 'often carries us beyond our
facile conceiving to seek the ground of our thinking. But he
does more. He confronts us repeatedly with an abyss. For
he strives to induce us to leap to new ground, to think in
fresh ways.' As an antidote to facile forms of conceiving,
Heidegger turns what goes without saying into an object of
inquiry itself:

> Being can be covered up so extensively that it becomes for-
> gotten and no question arises about it or about its meaning.
> Thus that which demands that it become a phenomenon,
> and which demands this in a distinctive sense and in terms
> of its ownmost content as a thing, is what phenomenology
> has taken into its grasp thematically as its object. (BT: 59)

In other words, the very thing (Being) that we take for
granted and assume as our starting point is, for Heidegger,
the principal concern of his phenomenological project. The
relevance of all this ontological rumination to the study of
the media rests upon the way in which Heidegger's search for
'the ground of our thinking' parallels the sort of structuring
processes we need to be sensitive to if we are to understand
properly the ground from which media mediate. Before we
can attempt to leap to 'new ground', however, there is the

abyss we need to cross – the gap in understanding that confronts such a radical project.

Whilst dismissive responses like that of Edwards are
extreme, such individual reactions stem from a recognizable
trait often associated with the wider Anglo-American philosophical tradition in which the scientific values of exactitude
and measurement are typically privileged over the ultimate
value that theorists like Heidegger place upon questioning.
Phrases such as 'glossogonous metaphysics' are therefore
more than merely a scathing critique of Heidegger's abstruse
expression. They are the result of an instinctive recoiling
at the scale and unashamedly non-empiricist nature of his
theoretical ambition, and, we might add, such name calling, which uses a similarly abstruse linguistic construction,
already betrays any purported commitment to empirical
fact-finding. Much more than name calling, however, it represents an evocatively florid manifestation of a substantial
(albeit somewhat latent and incompletely articulated) objection that goes beyond a mere complaint about style. This
deeper source of the objection comes from a long-standing
antipathy between the Anglo-American philosophical tradition and that mode of thinking that has come to be known as
Continental Philosophy, of which Heidegger is perhaps the
main spokesperson or 'poster child'.

2 The truth of Heidegger

This plethora of information can seduce us into failing to
recognize the real problem. We shall not get a genuine
knowledge of essences simply by the syncretistic activity
of universal comparison and classification. Subjecting the
manifold to tabulation does not ensure any actual understanding of what lies there before us as thus set in order. If
an ordering principle is genuine, it has its own content as a

thing [*Sachgehalt*], which is never to be found by means of such ordering, but is already presupposed in it. So if one is to put various pictures of the world in order, one must have an explicit idea of the world as such. And if the 'world' itself is something constitutive for Dasein, one must have insight into Dasein's basic structures in order to treat the world-phenomenon conceptually.

BT: 77

Belying criticisms of incomprehensibility, and read with due care and attention, the above statement provides us with a clear rationalè for the need to go beyond the conceptual limitations of a scientific outlook that, because of its deliberate constitution, is unable to deal in phenomenological essences that lie outside its self-imposed ordering scheme. For Heidegger, scientific methodology systematically and inevitably overlooks its own motivating impulse and is therefore innately unable to help us see what it already and necessarily takes for granted: 'Science only ever encounters that which its manner of representation has previously admitted as a possible object for itself' (BFL: 8). Rather than helping to find ways around this problem, the scientific mode of thought has become the de facto standard of intellectual enquiry through the institutionalization and fetishization of its reflexive blind spot. This occurs at the expense of thinkers like Heidegger for whom Being is the explicit concern rather than merely constituting a neutral container for beings/entities. It is the radical nature of Heidegger's distinctly ontological approach that acts as the plessor[1] that produces the knee-jerk reactions of Heidegger's most vehement critics.

In its general adherence to a 'social science' model of investigation, the field of Media and Communication Studies is dominated by pseudo-scientific aspirations and a consequent tendency to equate truth with terminological/empiricist exactitude. The result is that the full empirical subtlety of the lived experience of today's mediascape is sacrificed to the requirements of empiricist rigour. It is important to emphasize, at this early point, our deliberate use of the term *empiricist* rather than *empirical*. We use 'empiricist' to convey the mentality that reduces experience to what is objectifiable and measurable. By contrast, the empirical still includes that which exists but which may not lend itself to easy objectification or measurement. A quick illustration of this point is provided by the phenomenon of desire. Few readers, if any, would deny desire is a powerful part of human experience, but attempting to measure it betrays a misunderstanding of its essentially ineffable nature. In addition, desire is inherently positional; there needs to be a gap between desire and its object – by definition you cannot desire something you already have. Desire thus structures human experience indirectly but no less powerfully and in distinctly real, but very hard to quantify, ways. This is the sort of structuring role that media technologies play in contemporary life, the truth of which Heidegger's non-empiricist but rigorously empirical mode of thought is particularly well suited to demonstrate.

By stark contrast with the tautological tendencies of a social-science model only able to ascertain what it is, a priori, designed to reveal about mediated phenomena, Heidegger questions what we talk about, how we talk about it and why we talk about it. Whilst media and communications scholars typically displace essential value judgements with an unjustified assumption of instrumental neutrality, Heidegger begins by deliberately alienating things, instituting a kind of conceptual distance paradoxically at the point of obscene proximity. He does this by providing, for example, a close (for some, uncomfortably close) meditation on a seemingly mundane object like a jug and proceeds to render this simple and familiar object increasingly strange, unfamiliar and remote (TT). This procedure clearly cuts across the grain of what readers normally expect. The usual expectation of communication, whether it is a thoughtful meditation composed by a well-known philosopher or a tabloid newspaper story, is that the text should assist our understanding of something by taking what is strange or distant and making it more familiar and accessible. Heidegger recalibrates our understanding by doing the exact opposite. He takes what is nearest to us and shows how far we are from fully understanding it.

3 *Telepresence*

All distances in time and space are shrinking. Man now reaches overnight, by plane, places which formerly took weeks and months of travel. He now receives instant information, by radio, of events which he formerly only learned about only years later, if at all. The germination and growth of plants, which remained hidden throughout the seasons, is now exhibited publicly in a minute on film. Distant sites of the most ancient cultures are shown on film as if they stood this very moment amidst today's street traffic. Moreover, the film attests to what it shows by presenting also the camera and its operators at work. The peak of this abolition of every possibility of remoteness is reached by television, which will soon pervade and dominate the whole machinery of communication.

TT: 163

After three thousand years of explosion, by means of fragmentary and mechanical technologies, the Western world is imploding. During the mechanical age we had extended our bodies in space. Today, after more than a century of electric technology, we have extended our central nervous system itself in a global embrace, abolishing both space and time as far as our planet is concerned.

McLuhan 1995: 3

According to James Carey, there have been two competing definitions of communication operative in contemporary culture, 'a transmission view of communication and a ritual view of communication'. 'The transmission view of communication,' Carey (1989: 15) writes, 'is the commonest in our culture – perhaps in all industrial cultures – and it dominates contemporary dictionary entries under the term. It is defined by terms such as "imparting," "sending," "transmitting," or "giving information to others."' It is formed from a metaphor of geography or transportation. Although Heidegger mobilizes this common and dominant understanding of communication, he immediately complicates things. In his essay 'The Thing', for example, he explores the usually unproblematic notion of *closeness* in relation to the impact of media technologies. In doing so, he deploys a conceptualization of communication media very close to Marshall McLuhan's 'point of departure' in *Understanding Media* as can be seen in the juxtaposition of the two quotations above. For McLuhan (and later Baudrillard) and Heidegger, the defining feature of the post-war period was not found in the explosive force of the atom bomb, but rather in the *implosion* brought about in particular by the technologies of telecommunications. This implosive overcoming of distance and delay is what communication, strictly speaking, is all about.

According to Heidegger's paradoxical analysis, however, these innovations in the techniques and technologies of communication do not, as it is naturally assumed, bring everything near. Unlike McLuhan, whose thinking remains at the level of the conceptual opposition between the explosive nature of the atom bomb and the implosive nature of telecommunications, Heidegger thinks through and all the way down the implications of the eradication of distance – an eradication that would appear to be virtually complete in telepresence technology:

> Yet this frantic abolition of all distance brings no nearness; for nearness does not consist in shortness of distance. What is least remote from us in point of distance, by virtue of its picture on film or its sound on the radio, can remain far from us. What is incalculably far from us in point of distance can be near to us. Short distance is not in itself nearness. Nor is great distance remoteness. (TT: 165)

Thus, for Heidegger at least, obliteration of distance and delay – the shortening of geophysical space and time – does not result in the achievement of McLuhan's 'global village'.

In *Being and Time*, Heidegger's investigation of things begins with what is closest to us, those pieces of equipment that are always and already *ready-to-hand*. This is Heidegger's term (explored in detail in chapter 3) for the way the status of things change when they are experienced as technological objects. He explores how the specific properties of individual artefacts are subsumed by the overarching context from which they derive their full usage. For example, at the simplest level, a carpenter's chisel is used as part of a broader workshop and panoply of well-worn tools whereby the ready-to-hand is a literal description of the almost subconscious ease with which the carpenter reaches out for the necessary tool at a particular moment. At a much larger and sophisticated scale, ready-to-hand also describes objects like a jet airliner that only functions as part of a whole network of supporting technologies – runways, radar stations, fuelling systems and so on. This exploration of what constitutes a thing, and what then transforms a thing into a

ready-to-hand *object*, leads to a further fundamental questioning of how closeness to the entities we encounter is
configured.

Heidegger, in other words, distinguishes the mere
shrinking of distance affected by the implosive force of telecommunications from the nearness of things. The former
is, on his account, just shorter distances; the latter involves
a kind of intimacy and proximity that is not necessarily
dependent on or reducible to physical distance. It is, therefore, related to what Carey proposes as the 'ritual view'. For
Carey, this alternative conceptualization of communication
'exploits the ancient identity and common roots of the terms
"commonness," "communion," "community," and "communication"' (1989: 18). By characterizing things this way,
Carey appears to be channelling Heidegger; he performs an
etymological retrieval of an older, 'more original' definition
of the word 'communication' to give expression to a concept
of shared intimacy and proximity that is otherwise than the
closing of physical distance. Heidegger's analysis, therefore,
highlights a kind of tension or even paradox that defines the
contemporary mediated situation. Our 'concern', to use
the language of *Being and Time*, can now occur anytime, any-
place, anywhere (as an old advertisement for Martini put it).
But as Henry David Thoreau insightfully pointed out prior
to Heidegger:

> we are in great haste to construct a magnetic telegraph
> from Maine to Texas; but Maine and Texas, it may be, have
> nothing important to communicate. We are eager to tunnel
> under the Atlantic and bring the Old World some weeks
> nearer to the New; but perchance the first news that will
> leak through the broad, flapping American ear will be that
> the Princess Adelaide has the whooping cough. (Thoreau
> 1910: 67)

Everything appears to be coming closer together but the essence of the thing, what Heidegger in *Being and Time* called the 'thingness of the thing' (BT: 9), appears to be ever more remote, inaccessible and out of reach.

4 Technological determinism

Heidegger's name frequently appears in the list of authors who supported technological determinism. However, the question is not as clear as supposed.

Lucena 2009: 110

Technological determinism is a technology-led theory of social change that situates technical innovation as the *primum movens* of human history. The theory is usually credited to American sociologist Thorstein Veblen (Ellul 1964 [1954]: xviii; Jones 1990: 210), and it becomes something of a fixture in the fields of Media and Communication Studies through the work of individuals like Charles Horton Cooley (1962: 65), who once argued that 'we understand nothing rightly unless we perceive the manner in which the revolution in communication has made a new world for us', and the iconic twentieth-century media theorists Jacques Ellul (1964 [1954]), Harold Innis (1951) and Marshall McLuhan (1995). Although extremely influential, the theory is typically refuted by two other explanations concerning the relationship between technology and society – *sociocultural determinism* and *volunteerism*. According to David Chandler (1996: 2), the former 'presents technologies and media as entirely subordinate to their development and use in particular socio-political, historical, and culturally specific contexts'. The latter 'emphasizes individual control over the tools which they see themselves as "choosing" to use'. Both alternatives, therefore, deploy a version of what Heidegger calls 'the instrumental and anthropological definition of technology' (QCT: 5).

Heidegger, for his part, does not take sides in this arguably *ontic* debate. Instead, he advances a radical form of technological determinism that, following his essential commitment to ontological concerns, exceeds the conceptual grasp of the determinist/anti-determinist debate and, at the same time, constitutes the common ground that makes this debate possible in the first place. For this reason, we can say that Heidegger *deconstructs* technological determinism. Although 'deconstruction' or what is often misconstrued as 'the method of deconstructivism' is something usually attributed to the work of Jacques Derrida, Derrida has made it clear that this philosophical innovation is rooted in Heidegger's *destruktion* of metaphysics that was to have comprised the planned second part of *Being and Time*. 'When I choose this word [deconstruction]', Derrida (1991: 270–1) explained, 'or when it imposed itself upon me – I think it was in *Of Grammatology* – I little thought it would be credited with such a central role in the discourse that interested me at the time. Among other things I wished to translate and adapt to my own ends the Heideggerian word *Destruktion*.' Although a good deal of ink could be and has been spilled on this matter (see, for example, Gasche 1986: 109–20), we simply note two important aspects that will be useful for the chapters that follow.

First, the word 'deconstruction', to begin with a negative characterization, does not mean to take apart, to un-construct or to disassemble. Despite a popular misconception that has become something of an institutional (mal)practice, it is neither a form of destructive analysis, a kind of intellectual demolition, nor a process of reverse engineering. As Derrida (1988: 147) has described it, 'the de- of *de*construction signifies not the demolition of what is constructing itself, but rather what remains to be thought beyond the constructionist or destructionist schema.' For this reason, deconstruction is something entirely other than what is understood and delimited by the conceptual difference situated between, for example, 'construction' and its opposites.

Second, to put it in more positive terms, deconstruction comprises a general strategy by which to intervene in this and all other conceptual oppositions that have and continue to organize and regulate our systems of knowing. Towards this end, it involves, as Derrida described it, a double gesture of *inversion* and conceptual *displacement*:

> On the one hand, we must traverse a phase of *overturning*. To do justice to this necessity is to recognize that in a classical philosophical opposition we are not dealing with the peaceful coexistence of a *vis-à-vis*, but rather with a violent hierarchy. One of the two terms governs the other (axiologically, logically, etc.), or has the upper hand. To deconstruct the opposition, first of all, is to overturn the hierarchy at a given moment . . . That being said – and on the other hand – to remain in this phase is still to operate on the terrain of and from the deconstructed system. By means of this double, and precisely stratified, dislodged and dislodging, writing, we must also mark the interval between inversion, which brings low what was high, and the irruptive emergence of a new 'concept', a concept that can no longer be, and never could be, included in the previous regime. (Derrida 1981 [1972]: 41–3)

Heidegger's reformulation of technological determinism follows the contours of this 'double gesture'. He first sides with what many would consider the deprecated term in the determinism/anti-determinism debate. At times, it does sound as if Heidegger is simply and uncritically endorsing a strict technological determinist position:

> Technological advance will move faster and faster and can never be stopped. In all areas of his existence, man will be encircled ever more tightly by the forces of technology. The forces, which everywhere and every minute claim, enchain, drag along, press and impose upon man under the form of some technical contrivance or other – these forces, since man has not made them, have moved long since beyond his will and have outgrown his capacity for decision. (DOT: 51)

However, Heidegger does not stop at a mere endorsement of your standard, run-of-the-mill technological determinism. Instead of attending to the social consequences of individual technological artefacts or sophisticated technological systems, his thinking targets the essence of technology, which as he reminds us has little or nothing to do with actual technological contrivances, and the way that it contextualizes or *frames* a particular revealing of Being – a mode of disclosure that is definitive of the modern era. Consequently, if we continue to call this 'technological determinism', it is most certainly a form of determinism that is profoundly different from what is typically situated under this term. It is, as Derrida describes it, a new concept 'that can no longer be, and never could be, included in the previous regime' (Derrida 1981 [1972]: 43).

CONCLUSION

> Questioning builds a way . . . The way is a way of thinking. All ways of thinking, more or less perceptibly, lead through language in a manner that is extraordinary.
>
> QCT: 3

We have described a variety of reasons why reading Heidegger may alienate students and scholars of media. For example, the sort of knee-jerk rejection (the strength of which often implies an inappropriately emotional element) often caused because of the language he uses and his relentless commitment to questioning. However, it should be recognized that there are also those who struggle with his work in good faith because it is genuinely difficult to understand the idiom in which he writes, or, even if it is understood, to see the relevance of his approach for the media, given his apparent fixation with the nature of quite old-fashioned things rather than hi-tech communication gadgets. In response, we suggest that what makes reading Heidegger difficult, remote and inaccessible is, to a certain degree, an inevitable consequence of the manner by which his methods of presentation complement the needs of his subject matter. Heidegger is generally overlooked as a thinker who has a high degree of relevance to media because a series of steps need to be taken to perceive that relevance. These include an appreciation that:

- His probing analysis of deceptively simple objects like hammers, jugs, paintings, etc. is actually based on an essential sense of environment and positionality that, in what it tells us ontologically about the structural relationships of Being, brings a new and profound depth of understanding to *mediated* being.
- His analysis marries form and content such that in order to understand the structure of Being in a radically new fashion, the necessary critical and perspectival distance for that understanding is achieved through the development of a correspondingly radical mode of language.

Consequently, a hypersensitive response to Heidegger's purported lack of superficial intelligibility misses the essential

point – this very difficulty is necessary if we are to understand fully a mediated environment, the experience of which
normally goes without being recognized as such. For that
reason, whilst this book seeks to foreclose the distance the
reader experiences by making Heidegger's thinking more
accessible and approachable, it still needs to be recognized
that Heidegger's own mode of communication resists this
effort and pushes things in the opposite direction. From the
first pages of *Being and Time*, which sought to rehabilitate
the question of Being, Heidegger takes what is seemingly
familiar and immediately accessible and endeavours to
make it increasingly remote, strange and question-worthy.
Consequently, he deliberately counters and works against the
usual expectation of media as arbiters (*media*tors) of distance,
difference and delay. If the reader of Heidegger continues
to cling to conventional expectations, under the assumption
that there is always and everywhere a correct understanding
beyond reproach, then she will struggle to understand the
truth of what he does or why he does it.

1

WE NEED TO TALK ABOUT MEDIA

INTRODUCTION: SPEAKING OF MEDIA

To write about media is to raise the question of what gives writing the presumption to speak for other media. Language presents itself as the meta-medium to contain all past and future media.

Adilkno 1998: 7

In what way does language occur as language? We answer: Language speaks.

LAN: 190

To say anything about media, we inevitably find ourselves needing to use some form of media. We are, therefore, already engaged in and with media. In this endeavour, language has a privileged status. It is, as Adilkno – the Dutch foundation for the advancement of illegal knowledge – points out above, the meta-medium in which all other media, past or future, are contained, reflected and represented. For this reason, language is widely considered the *first* medium of human communication, 'first' in chronological terms in so far as it was the initial means of providing for human information exchange and communicative interaction that went beyond the gestural.[1] 'First' also in terms of status in so far as every other medium – writing, print, radio, film, television, internet, etc. – is subsequent to, serves to extend the reach of and is dependent upon the facility of language. So far so good; all of this seems uncontroversial. Heidegger, however, asks a further penetrating question about how language actually occurs and suggests that, whilst we assume it is we who speak language, it is language that also speaks us.

This seemingly counter-intuitive formulation is an example of what we repeatedly argue throughout the subsequent chapters is a central feature of Heidegger's importance as a thinker – the persistence with which he fundamentally questions conventional assumptions of the most basic sort. It is therefore fitting that this first chapter initiates our exploration of the way Heidegger's work challenges those taken-for-granted assumptions we make about media by using language to go right to the root of all media. Heidegger undertakes an inquiry into the essential nature of language, 'by means of a relentless pursuit of whatever it is that our path's formula indicates when it says: To bring language as language to language' (WTL: 399). In this pithy but puzzling formula one sees a good example of why Heidegger's mode of thought is so useful for, *pace* McLuhan, understanding the media. In his analysis of language, Heidegger directly reflects on how we conceptualize the very thing we use for the act of conceptualizing. This chapter, therefore, shows how this reflexive mode of thinking about language as a medium is a particularly useful conceptual resource for better appreciating what we normally take for granted about the media because it happens so unobtrusively and ubiquitously.

The conclusion that language constitutes the principal means or fundamental instrument of human expression and communication seems to be entirely correct. In fact, the very effort to articulate this point already supplies what looks to be ample and seemingly irrefutable evidence of the claim itself. It is so clear and has been so widely accepted that it appears to be beyond question or in need of argumentation. Who would ever deny this? Who would ever question these things? Who would ever say that language is not first and foremost a means by which to say something? Well . . . Heidegger for one. He not only contests the conventional understanding of language as an instrument or medium of human expression but also rejects the seemingly incontrovertible evidence that it is human beings who solely possess and use language. 'In accordance with its essence,' Heidegger writes, '*language* is neither expression nor a matter of human manipulation. *Language speaks*' (LAN: 197). Like the previous notion of bringing language to language as language, the idea that "language speaks" represents a distinctly Heideggerian quality to which we will keep returning – Heidegger's ability to use his own language to encapsulate and convey seemingly puzzling ideas that encourage and help us to reflect upon the nature of media and acts of mediated representation in their most essential sense.

THE MEDIUM OF REPRESENTATION: INSTRUMENTAL AND CONSTITUTIVE LANGUAGE

I want to suggest, to play on the Gospel of St. John, that in the beginning was the word; words are not names for things but, to steal a line from Kenneth Burke, things are the signs

of words. Reality is not given, not humanly existent, independent of language and toward which language stands as
a pale refraction. Rather reality is brought into existence, is
produced, by communication – by, in short, the construction, apprehension, and utilization of symbolic forms.

Carey 1989: 25

Language is the house of Being in which man ek-sists by
dwelling.

LOH: 213

Language, in one way or another, was, and continued to be,
one of the principal concerns of Heidegger's thinking, from
the period before *Being and Time* (1927) to the Le Thor and
Zähringen seminars delivered just a few years prior to his
death in 1976. The theme's persistent presence, however,
should not be taken to mean that Heidegger had a single
univocal view of language that remained unchanged from the
beginning to the end of his philosophical career. Although
language was a crucial issue for Heidegger's thinking, what
he thought about it evolved and developed considerably.
Charles Guignon, for example, argues that Heidegger's view
of language in *Being and Time* appears to be pulled in two
apparently opposite directions – an instrumental versus a
constitutive viewpoint.

The instrumentalist view, exemplified in the work of
Wilhelm Dilthey, considers language to be a kind of tool or
instrument of human expression:

From the instrumentalist's standpoint, our ability to use
language is grounded in some prior grasp of the nonseman-
tic significance of the contexts in which we find ourselves.
It is only because we have first understood the nature of
reality that we can then come to comprehend the meaning

of words. Language is seen as a tool for communicating and ordering this prior grasp of reality. (Guignon 1983: 117–18)

The constitutive view, or what has also been called 'linguistic constitutionalism' (Wrathall 2011: 122), represents an opposing position. According to this interpretation, language is not a tool or instrument that is used to communicate information about some pre-existing reality; it is what shapes and makes this reality possible in the first place. In other words, words do not merely represent things as some derived and pale reflection of what is. Instead, words constitute the reality of things. Or as James Carey cleverly describes it by way of Kenneth Burke, 'words are not names for things but . . . things are the signs of words.'

Understood instrumentally, language is determined to be a set of available or ready-to-hand words, the totality of which would be contained in a dictionary and which can be organized and combined in order to say something intelligible about the world – a world that presumably exists and had been presented prior to its becoming re-presented in language. In other words, there is a real world – the way things really are – and then subsequent to this there is language, which is a tool that enables us to say something about this world by formulating representations of it in words that are more or less accurate. This common and seemingly intuitive understanding of language matches an equally common conceptualization of media as an instrument of communication. According to this way of thinking, it is assumed that there is an independent pre-existing reality of things, people and events. This real world is then subsequently re-presented, literally made present again, by various kinds of media – newspapers, books, photographs, radio transmissions, television documentaries, internet documents, video recordings, etc. – which are, on this account, a kind of secondary and derived image of what was initially present in the 'real world'.

Philosophically speaking, this view was first articulated and developed in the final book of Plato's *Republic*, where Socrates proposes an image by which to examine and explain the nature of representation. The image consists of three kinds of artisans and their products, in this case, home furnishings, specifically couches. At the apex, Socrates locates the εἶδος (*eidos*), the real and true form that is originally created by a deity. Subordinate to this, he situates a first-order representation, which is produced through the artistry of the craftsman. The craftsman, Socrates reasons, produces his creation by looking to and following the information provided by the form of the original thing (Plato 1987: 596b). The derived product of the craftsman is subsequently copied by the painter who creates not a couch per se but the mere appearance of a couch (Plato 1987: 596e). Although the craftsman copies the original εἶδος, the name 'imitator' or 'copier' is reserved for the painter, for as Glaucon, Socrates' interlocutor, argues, 'he is the imitator of the thing which the others produce' (Plato 1987: 597e). For this reason, imitation is situated in a phenomenal product that is at least three removes from the true and original reality of things.

According to this schema, the value of an image – whether it is made up of descriptive words, oil paint on canvas, or, for our more contemporary purposes, a rapid succession of individual photographs, or 3-D images on an HD monitor screen – comes to be assessed on the basis of its attention to, and ability to re-present the real, or its 'realism'. Relying on this illustration, Socrates eventually proposes two alternatives for dealing with mediated representation. Either the image and the various image-makers need to be expelled from the city, for, as he proposes, 'it is a deception and corruption of the mind' (Plato 1987: 595b), or this effort must be carefully used and regulated as a tool capable of serving and representing the real and true nature of things as they really are. To put it in today's terminology, this means either outright censorship or a kind of professional practice that espouses the standard journalistic values of 'objectivity' and 'fair and balanced' representations.

The constitutive view of language inverts the instrumentalist perspective. Instead of representing an independent and pre-existing real world, language and other forms of communication produce what we understand as our world and initially bring it into existence. In this case, the question is not, to borrow a statement Heidegger makes at the end of the Beiträge (CTP: 393), 'how does language relate to being?' but 'how does being relate to language?' Although this may sound counter-intuitive, it is a notion that has gained considerable traction in the latter half of the twentieth century. In the *Tractatus Logico-Philosophicus*, for instance, Ludwig Wittgenstein (1995 [1922]: 5.6) famously argued that 'the limits of my language mean the limits of my world.' In other words, the world I know and operate in is shaped, formed and contained by the words that I have at my disposal. Similar positions are advanced in what linguists call the Sapir-Whorf hypothesis, which in its strong form argues that the language one speaks determines one's social reality (Sapir 1941 [1929]: 162); in Peter Berger and Thomas Luckmann's *The Social Construction of Reality* (1966), which proposes that language and other symbolic forms construct the reality in which human beings live and operate; and Jean Baudrillard's *Simulations* (1983 [1981]: 1), in which he famously argued (by way of reference to a short story by Jorge-Luis Borges) that 'the territory no longer precedes the map, nor does it survive it. It is nevertheless the map that precedes the territory – precession of simulacra – it is the map that engenders the territory.'

In *Being and Time*, Heidegger mobilizes and differentiates the instrumental and constitutive views of language by distinguishing between what he calls language and *Rede*, which has typically been translated as 'talk' or 'discourse'. For Heidegger, discourse is the more fundamental aspect; it is the 'existential-ontological foundation of language' (BT: 203). Formulated in this way, talk has a constitutive function. It is not an instrument useful for making representations of the world; it is the principal mode of the world's disclosure, that by which entities come to show themselves in the first place. Language, by contrast, is how discourse gets expressed. It is, as Heidegger describes it, 'a totality of words [and] as an entity within-the-world, this totality thus becomes something which we may come across as ready-to-hand' (BT: 204). This means that 'language', at least as far as Heidegger uses this term in *Being and Time*, is considered to be an instrument for expressing what had been initially disclosed in and by discourse.[2] If, as Guignon argues, the earlier Heidegger was pulled in two different directions regarding this issue, it is his use of *Rede* or discourse that designates the constitutive interpretation and language that indicates instrumentalism.

The constitutive/instrumental distinction is not just an academic insight that is of interest to a small number of philosophers, linguists and sociologists. It is something we all know and understand from our everyday experience and encounter with media – whether the one-to-many form of traditional mass media or the many-to-many model of the internet and social media applications on our mobile devices. Many of the things that occur in our world, like a violent street protest on the other side of the globe, are not available to us in some immediate and direct form. What we know of these events and what we can say about them is something that is initially formed, shaped or determined by the

mediated representations that come to us through stories
and information published in newspapers, reports presented
on television news programmes, or user-produced information accessed over the internet by way of Twitter, Facebook
or other Web 2.0 applications. In these cases, we might think
that these media are merely representing events on the other
side of the world, but they are, in fact, creating for us the
very reality we think they merely represent.

COMMUNICATION AND DISCOURSE

> 'There is nothing outside the text.' That does not mean
> that all referents are suspended, denied, or enclosed in a
> book, as people have claimed, or have been naïve enough
> to believe and to have accused me of believing. But it does
> mean that every referent, all reality has the structure of a
> differential trace, and that one cannot refer to this 'real'
> except in an interpretive experience.
>
> Derrida 1993: 148

Derrida himself takes issue with the common misreading
of his now (in)famous statement, *il n'y a pas de hors-texte*
(there is nothing outside the text) (1976 [1967]: 158). He
makes explicitly clear that this statement does not mean that
everything is contained in a book such that the 'real world'
of existing things is nothing more than a fiction. Rather, he
is pointing out that linguistic signs and the other means of
communication are not some secondary phenomenon that
are added onto a more primordial and immediate experience of things. *Il n'y a pas de hors-texte* means that language
and mediated representations of all kinds are inextricably
bound up with how reality is disclosed to us. World disclosure [*Erschlossenheit*] is a related Heideggerian concept that
emphasizes the extent to which our experience of reality is

inevitably context-dependent rather than being a simple case of direct correspondence between the observer and neutral, objective phenomena (a theme developed in detail in chapter 2).

In specific relation to language, this point is further underlined by considering how it is already encoded and manifest in the very material of the words we use to describe it. 'Immediacy' is the term that is typically employed to identify that kind of direct experience of things outside language and beyond the influence of mediation. We say, for example, that there is a direct and immediate encounter with things prior to and in advance of our making mediated representations of it – first in language and then via other media. It should be noted, however, that the word 'immediacy' is formed by adding the negative prefix 'im-' to the root word 'media'. So in terms of the very word itself, 'immediacy' is derived from 'media' and understood as its negative counterpart. Mediation, in other words, is the original and normative state of things and the immediate is only formed by way of negating what is always and already available by way of mediation. This means that what is said about language in *Being and Time* does not necessarily result from Heidegger being torn between instrumentalist and constitutivist perspectives as Guignon argued. Instead, what Heidegger describes (in and by language) is the fact that what is called 'language' can be seen and must be properly understood according to both instrumentalist and constitutivist viewpoints and this necessitates a much more complex and nuanced understanding of communication than is normally allowed for within Communication Studies.

Since the groundbreaking work of Claude Shannon and Warren Weaver during and shortly after the Second World War, the dominant characterization of communication has been one of a dyadic process by which a message selected at

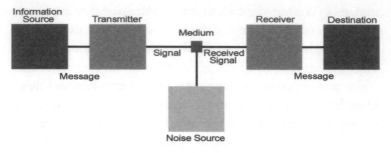

Figure 1.1   Shannon and Weaver's Model of Communication

an information source, or sender, is encoded and conveyed by means of some channel or transmission medium to a destination, or receiver (Figure 1.1). Understood in this way, communication is defined as the process of conveying information or the passing of messages from senders to receivers. And the fundamental task or problem of communication has been defined as 'reproducing at one point either exactly or approximately a message selected at another point' (Shannon and Weaver 1963: 31). This intentionally schematic characterization is stated in terms that are general enough to be able to describe everything from human speech to advanced technology, like the internet. 'When I talk to you,' Weaver (Shannon and Weaver 1963: 7) writes in his introduction, 'my brain is the information source, yours the destination; my vocal system is the transmitter, and your ear . . . is the receiver.' Likewise, in the case of email; my computer is the information source, the packet-switched network is the medium of message transmission, and your computer is the destination or receiver.

While much of Communication Studies has moved on from a simple transmission model and sets itself the scholarly task of highlighting the various complications and distortions that occur within any 'simple' act of communication (e.g. the 'noise' that may interrupt communication and, even if received, the different ways various receivers can then choose to decode the message, etc.) much of the discipline still works (even if only implicitly) with the Shannon and Weaver model. Communication Studies, in other words, recognizes that the transmission model describes an idealized form of a neutral process of communication which is subsequently complicated, in practical day-to-day terms, by various exigencies, disturbances and blockages. No serious communication scholar, for instance, would see the role of journalist as one in which information is unproblematically conveyed to the populace. However, at its best, and making suitable allowances for the myriad obstacles it faces, journalism is essentially understood as a profession that is guided by the aim of transmitting accurate or truthful information.

Heidegger, by contrast, rejects both the explicit and implicit conceptualizations of communication as an essentially neutral process organized around the most efficient form of information transmission. He argues instead for a much broader ontologically based interpretation that fundamentally questions the notion of communication as the passing of messages and the imparting of information to others even in an ideal setting with all possible barriers removed. According to Heidegger 'communication is never anything like a conveying of experiences, such as opinions or wishes, from the interior of one subject into the interior of another' (BT: 205). This effort, Heidegger argues, is actually a derived and specific case of a more general form of communication that is associated not with what occurs in and by language but rather with that articulation of Being that Heidegger calls discourse – that is, a common mode of disclosure rather than just information transmission. For this reason, communication is not, at least principally, the transmittal of data or messages from a sender to a receiver; it is first and foremost a co-state-of-mind that is shared with others.

'It is letting someone see with us what we have pointed out by way of giving it a definite character' (BT: 197).

Heidegger's interpretation emphasizes the common (the etymological root of the word 'communication') understanding of Being that necessarily precedes and initially makes possible the much more limited sense of communication as the process of message exchange or the conveying of experiences from one individual to another. Consequently, there are two senses of or two ways to consider communication. There is the primordial sense of the term that Heidegger associates with original disclosure and that he later identifies with the phrase 'existentiell communication' [*existentielle Mitteilung*] (BPP: 297), and there is a derived sense that could, following Heidegger's characterization of language in *Being and Time*, be called 'linguistic communication'. For James Carey, one of the relatively few communication scholars who explicitly acknowledged Heidegger's influence, these two aspects are expressed in terms of two different viewpoints concerning communication – a transmission and ritual view. The transmission view, like the process model of communication described and theorized by Shannon and Weaver, concerns the sending of messages or the imparting of information to others. The ritual view, by contrast, is actually older and, as Heidegger would characterize it, more primordial. 'In a ritual definition,' Carey (1989: 18) explains, 'communication is linked to terms such as "sharing," "participation," "association," "fellowship," and "the possession of a common faith."' This definition exploits the common etymological root of words like 'communication', 'community', 'communion' and 'commonness' – a commonality that is grounded in the very concept of the common. A similar formulation is contained within Emile Durkheim's anthropological notion of the collective effervescence experienced in religious services (Durkheim 2008 [1912]) and in works like *The Ecstasy of Communication* (1988 [1987]), Baudrillard's characterization of the parodic co-optation of this collective effervescence in its contemporary recast, simulated, media form.

Principally concerned as it is with message encoding and transfer, the transmission view focuses attention on questions concerning efficiency and effect rather than affect. As Mark Poster (1995: 25) describes it, 'the question to ask is how much information with how little noise may be transmitted at what speed and over what distance to how many locations?' These are precisely the kind of questions made possible and addressed by Shannon and Weaver's mathematical model, which sought to develop modes of measurement by which to quantify the efficiency of data transfer and the effectiveness of information transmission. 'If one examines a newspaper,' Carey (1989: 20) writes mobilizing a distinctly last-century example, 'under a transmission view of communication, one sees the medium as an instrument for disseminating news and knowledge, sometimes divertissement, in larger and larger packages over greater distances.' And the questions that such a view makes possible are limited mainly to matters of quantity, e.g. the amount and speed by which messages circulate over geographic distance, or quality, e.g. signal-to-noise ratio.

The ritual view enables an entirely different way of looking at things. 'A ritual view of communication,' Carey argues, 'will focus on a different range of problems in examining a newspaper. It will, for example, view reading a newspaper less as sending or gaining information and more as attending a mass, a situation in which nothing new is learned but in which a particular view of the world is portrayed and confirmed' (Carey 1989: 20). The ritual view, therefore, is concerned not with information transmission but with the discursive dimension of communication whereby a particular shared understanding of Being is first made available and disclosed. In other words, 'we do not', to return to Carey's newspaper example, 'encounter questions about the effect or functions of messages as such, but the role of presentation and involvement in the structuring of the reader's life and time' (Carey 1989: 21). If we were to update Carey's explanation for the digital age, the best example would probably be massively multi-player online role playing games, or MMORPGs. From a transmission viewpoint, the operative question for these internet-based applications is the speed at which data packets can be delivered through the network and processed by the end-user's system. From a ritual perspective, however, the important questions concern the common experience that such games create for users, namely, the production and maintenance of a shared, albeit virtual, reality. Although Carey takes up and extends Heidegger's innovative understanding of communication, demonstrating how it provides for a more nuanced understanding of media and its social significance, Heidegger already and pre-emptively complicates the picture. This is immediately evident in his analysis of *Gerede* or 'idle talk'.

IDLE TALK AND THE REAL DICTATORSHIP OF DAS MAN: TWITTER AVANT LA LETTRE

> The expression 'idle talk' is not used here in a 'disparaging' signification. Terminologically, it signifies a positive phenomenon which constitutes the kind of Being of everyday Dasein's understanding and interpreting.
>
> BT: 211

The term *Gerede* (derived from *Rede*) is commonly understood in colloquial German as 'gossip' or 'rumour', and rendered as 'idle talk' in standard English translations of *Being and Time*. Idle talk is, according to Heidegger, the way that human beings initially come into and experience language. It is, therefore, despite initial appearances, not necessarily a negative or pejorative term. Thus understood, idle talk performs an important function; it provides an already available context in which things have names and are nominally understood and interpreted as such. However, despite Heidegger's claim that idle talk is not a term of disparagement, it is difficult to take him at his word. This is because in subsequent sections of *Being and Time* he produces a sustained critique of the qualitative difference between what transpires in discursive talk (*Rede*) and what happens with idle talk (*Gerede*) and this critique, notwithstanding his own denial, further reinforces the disparagement already implied in the 'idle' part of the concept.

In the case of discursive talk, Wrathall explains, interlocutors actually 'pick up what is being communicated to each other, they are made ready for engagement with people and things in the world by sharing with each other a mode of understanding, a comportment toward common things we encounter in the world, as well as disposedness or a sense for the way things matter'. In idle talk, by contrast, 'something gets communicated but in such a way that the parties cannot successfully participate in a shared orientation toward things in the world' (Wrathall 2011: 111). Idle talk, therefore, identifies a kind of pointless chit-chat that circulates widely but actually says little or nothing. It is not so much a matter of understanding what is talked about but merely listening to what has been said in the talk as such. It is worth observing the essential similarity of this sentiment with Marshall McLuhan's famous aphorism, 'the medium is the message'.

Heidegger's concept of idle talk is particularly prescient, given the advent of narrowcasting applications like Facebook and Twitter, but to the extent that Heidegger's work has been addressed within Communication Studies, it has mainly been limited to the previous paradigm of broadcast media. In *Radio, Television, and Modern Life* (1996), for example, Paddy Scannell uses *Dasein*'s inherent quality of everydayness to explore broadcasting's 'world-disclosing function', but, failing to mention idle talk, Scannell uses Heidegger's ontology to support an enthusiastically positive interpretation of the media's cultural purpose: 'Classic social theory took a disenchanted view of a world that it found to be disenchanted . . . The kind of theory presented in this book finds the world (and in particular the world of broadcasting) as enchanted and enchanting, meaningful and full of meaning' (Scannell 1996: 21). Contra Scannell, considering the relationship between idle talk and the mass media makes the use of Heidegger's ontological perspective to support a sense of television's enchantment deeply problematic. This more critical interpretation of the mass medium of broadcast television is contained within the collection of essays titled *RIU|A|TV? Heidegger and the Televisual*. In this book's short afterword, Mark Jackson draws a distinction between *television* and the *televisual*: 'If we imagine that *television* names that receptivity of pure intuition and the spontaneity of authentic speech, the *televisual* names its classical opposition, the inauthentic as *Gerede*, rumor, arbitrary pronouncement, the circulation of idle talk' (Jackson in Fry 1993: 118).

Idle talk is indeed a natural part of *Dasein*'s everydayness, and whilst everydayness itself is also a constitutive part of what Heidegger calls our 'thrownness' into the world, it is hard to escape Heidegger's clearly articulated sense that, constituting the currency of newspapers, gossip magazines, broadcasting and so on, idle talk is part of a much wider environment permeated by a *Dasein*-debilitating sense of averageness: 'In utilizing public means of transport and in making use of information services such as the newspaper,

every Other is like the next. This Being-with-one-another
dissolves one's own *Dasein* completely into the kind of
Being of "the Others".... In this inconspicuousness and
unascertainability, the real dictatorship of the "they" [*das
Man*] is unfolded.' (BT: 164) Thus, everyday *Dasein* – what
Heidegger associates with the experience of an anonymous
'they' or *das Man* – is enthralled by the seemingly ceaseless
noise of public chit-chat and in the process distracted from
engaging in the effort of genuine 'existentiell communication'. In a passage that could be applied to any media ranging
from the daily newspapers to the internet and mobile apps,
Heidegger suggests that idle talk 'is something which anyone
can rake up; it not only releases one from the task of genuinely understanding, but develops an undifferentiated kind
of intelligibility, for which nothing is closed off any longer.'
(BT: 213) Dwight MacDonald expresses a similar point
(albeit more acerbically):

> Consider Life, a typical homogenized mass-circulation
> magazine ... Its contents are as thoroughly homogenized
> as its circulation. The same issue will contain a serious
> exposition of atomic theory alongside a disquisition on Rita
> Hayworth's love life; photos of starving Korean children
> picking garbage from the ruins of Pusan and of sleek models
> wearing adhesive brassieres ... nine colors of Renoirs plus
> a memoir by his son, followed by a full-page picture of a
> roller-skating horse. (MacDonald in Rosenberg and White
> 1957: 62)

It is this 'undifferentiated kind of intelligibility' that leads
Siegfried Kracauer to observe: 'The monotony of this hodge-
podge is the just revenge for its inconsequentiality, which is
heightened by the thoughtless way the individual sequences
are combined into a mosaic' (1995 [1963]: 311). This is the

mass media's particular contribution to how, more generally, technology confronts *Dasein*, and it is this general lack
of differentiation that distinguishes idle talk from genuine
discourse.

Heidegger's criticism, therefore, runs unfashionably
against the Zeitgeist. It is often simply assumed that access
to greater amounts of data in shorter periods of time is what
ultimately counts and makes a difference. This assumption is
underwritten by Shannon and Weaver's process model and
supported by the transmission view of communication that
it endorses. It is promoted in the marketing rhetoric of tele-
communication service providers, which promises unlimited
access to more information at ever-increasing speeds, even
though the more information we receive, the more it seems
we hear and see the same stuff. With more 24-hour news
channels available on cable television, more web sites and
blogs with real-time updates and more mobile apps to access
and download information on the go, what we get is not necessarily news but a seemingly endless stream of chit-chat, the
newness (and newsworthiness) of which is extremely doubt-
ful. Or as Peter Sloterdijk (1987 [1983]: 312–13), following
this line of thought, has argued, 'the media can provide
everything because they have given up without a trace the
ambition of philosophy to also understand the given. They
comprise everything because they comprehend nothing.
They talk about everything and say nothing about anything.
The media kitchen serves us daily a reality stew with innu-
merable ingredients, but it still tastes the same every day.'

At the same time, however, we need to recognize that
Heidegger's indictment can itself be accused of reiterating
and reproducing a critique of media technology that has been
in circulation since at least the time of Plato's *Phaedrus*, in
which the act of writing was denounced – in and by writing –
as a harbinger of doom for the established oral tradition and

dominant form of culture. The problem with this particular approach is that it seems to call upon and reproduce the already available philosophical gossip or chit-chat regarding media. In David Dwan's words, 'Heidegger's pronouncements about mass communications are, it seems, banal in themselves and partake in the very idle talk he professes to despise' (2003: 114). In order to assess whether Heidegger's pronouncements are indeed banal, we need to examine further the relationship between the act of mediation (whether it be via language or technology) and our uniquely linguistic mode of existence.

LANGUAGE AND 'LANGUAGE'[3]: MEDIATION AND THE OPENNESS TO BEING

In the current view, language is held to be a kind of communication. It serves for verbal exchange and agreement, and in general for communicating. But language is not only and not primarily about an audible and written expression of what is to be communicated. It not only puts forth in words and statements what is overtly or covertly intended to be communicated; language alone brings what is, as something that is, into the Open for the first time. Where there is no language, as in the being of stone, plant, and animal, there is also no openness of what is, and consequently no openness either of that which is not and of the empty.

(OWA: 73)

The pivot between what is routinely called the early and the late Heidegger is a perceived alteration in approach and thinking that is called 'the turn', or *die Kehre*. Although there remains considerable debate about the exact nature and significance of this 'turn' (on this issue, see Richardson 2003 and Sheehan 2001), one thing that is not debated is the fact that 'language', which had been of marginal interest in the project of *Being and Time*, begins to take centre-stage in the texts of the mid-1930s and beyond. After the turn, therefore, language not only becomes an explicit subject for Heidegger's thinking but what he thinks about language also appears to be subject to a kind of transformation that centres less on what it transmits than what it discloses. This crucial distinction goes straight to the heart of the relationship media have to *Dasein* portrayed by Heidegger as the mode of disclosure experienced in human Being. This focus on disclosure conceived as openness is evident in the above excerpt from what is considered to be one of Heidegger's pivotal texts of the mid-1930s, 'The Origin of the Work of Art'.

There are at least two things to note in this informative passage. First, Heidegger uses the term 'language' in such a way that it appears to name both the means of expression and the original disclosure/mediation of Being. Language is, Heidegger emphasizes, not only the audible and written means of expression, but it is also and primarily that which brings things into the openness of disclosure in the first place. Unlike *Being and Time*, therefore, this text does not make a terminological distinction between 'language' as the instrumental means of expression and 'discourse', or *Rede*, as a form of primordial disclosure. In fact, one symptom of the shift in Heidegger's thinking after the turn is the almost absolute absence of the term *Rede*, which had been so crucial to the analysis of *Being and Time*. After the turn, we can say, Heidegger no longer talks about talk.

Second, the significance of this can be interpreted in at least two different ways. It has been, on the one hand, read as an indicator of a major shift in Heidegger's thinking. 'The standard interpretation of Heidegger,' Wrathall (2011: 123) explains, 'seems to go like this: the early Heidegger was not a linguistic constitutionalist, but at some point during the notorious "turning" in his philosophy, he became one.' This is the case, for example, with Cristina Lafont's *Heidegger, Language and World-Disclosure* (2000 [1994]) where it is argued that Heidegger ultimately articulates a kind of linguistic idealism:

> He [Heidegger] will declare language to be the court of appeal that (as the 'house of being') judges beforehand what can be encountered within the world. With this reification of the world-disclosing function of language, what things are becomes thoroughly dependent on what is contingently 'disclosed' for a *historical linguistic community through a specific language*. Thus, the world-disclosure that is contained in a given language becomes the final authority for judging the intraworldly knowledge that this world-disclosure has made possible in the first place. (Lafont 2000 [1994]: 7, emphasis in the original)

Formulated in this way, language is originally disclosive. It not only shapes and determines the entities that are encountered in the world but, because 'language' on this reading is understood as a specific human language – like German, ancient Greek, or Latin – what is able to be disclosed varies across different linguistic communities. This means, then, that different languages enable and disclose different kinds of entities, or at least different ways of framing and revealing what is and comes into being. This is not just an abstract theoretical insight, it is something that is actually put into practice by Heidegger's own mode of expression that his critics frequently dislike. He is (in)famous for locating and employing foreign words, like the ancient Greek term λογος (logos), precisely because they are able to point out and disclose something that is not able to be accessed by way of the translated terms, like ratio, reason, logic or rationality.

Heidegger employs these 'foreign' words not just to be cute, clever or scholarly; he does so because they provide privileged access to something that is unique and specific to what has been disclosed in and by a particular language.

This interpretation, however, may be seen as taking things too far. According to Wrathall (2011: 124), 'something does indeed change after "the turn", but the shift is in large part a change in thinking about what the word "language" names, and thus it cannot be reduced to a simple change of view about the role of language in mediating our access to the world or in constituting the world.' On Wrathall's reading there are at least two senses that Heidegger provides for the general term 'language' – originary language and ordinary language (Wrathall 2011: 155). Ordinary language is what had been called 'language' in *Being and Time*. It entails, as Heidegger explains, in an essay titled 'Language', three related assumptions:

1 Language is, first and foremost, a kind of expression, literally the 'pressing out' of internal states of mind into some kind of external surface manifestation.
2 Language is regarded as a human activity. 'Accordingly we have to say that man speaks, and that he always speaks some language.'
3 This 'human expression is always a presentation and representation of the real and the unreal'. (LAN: 192)

This characterization, as Heidegger is quick to point out, is not incorrect. 'No one,' he writes, 'would dare to declare incorrect, let alone reject as useless, the identification of language as audible utterance of inner emotions, as human activity, as a representation by image and by concept. The view of language thus put forth is correct, for it conforms to what an investigation of linguistic phenomena can make out in them at any time' (LAN: 192). But this ordinary view of language, which is, it should be recalled, nothing less than a restatement of linguistic instrumentalism, does not necessarily exhaust what is meant by 'language'.

Beyond this instrumental aspect, language also works at the deeper or more primordial level of the logos whereby entities are first disclosed as such and brought out of concealment and into the open. This other, more primordial aspect of language Wrathall calls 'originary language' because it is what makes entities as such available in their being. It is this aspect that *Being and Time* had sought, perhaps rather incompletely, to articulate with the term *Rede*, and it is this originary dimension that Heidegger, since at least the time of the mid-1930s, associates with poetry. 'The essence of language,' Heidegger (LET: 141) states in the conclusion to a 1934 lecture course on logic,

> announces itself, not where it is misused and levelled, distorted, and forced into a means of communication, and sunken down into mere expression of a so-called interior. The essence of language essences where it happens as world-forming power, that is, where it in advance performs and brings into jointure the being of beings. The original language is the language of poetry.[4]

Objections to Heidegger's work by analytical philosophers frequently focus on this recourse to non-analytical language. For Heidegger, however, a unique quality of poetic language is the way in which, in its very form, it enables us to attend to the medium of language itself and how that medium mediates.

According to Wrathall, then, 'Language', as the term is used in the texts of the later Heidegger, admits of two different aspects. Characterized in this fashion, the difference between what Wrathall calls 'originary language' and 'ordinary language' continues to develop what Heidegger had initially sought to describe in *Being and Time*. The turn in Heidegger's thinking is therefore not so much a revolutionary change as it is an evolutionary development or maturation. Furthermore, the distinction between originary and ordinary language helps make sense of that notoriously disorientating statement: 'Language speaks.' By this Heidegger does not necessarily seek to oppose the ordinary view of language as human expression. Instead, this statement indicates that language, in its originary dimension, first provides access to the being of entities and that ordinary language – the language that is spoken or used by human beings – is less something we choose to do and more something through which we partake of our human being in the first place: 'Language speaks. Man speaks insofar as he corresponds to language' (LAN: 210). In other words, language originally speaks, and we, in speaking ordinary language, seek to respond to and take responsibility for what had been originally spoken in and by language. In specific relation to the media, however, this raises the question of what taking responsibility may mean for not only what we say, but also how we may be spoken by the mediating language that we speak.

TWO VERSIONS OF AN ANTI-REALISM

So I renounce and sadly see:
Where the word breaks off, no thing may be.
    Stephan George, 'The Word', 1919; quoted in NOL: 60

To recap, there are at least two competing interpretations of language in the later Heidegger, both of which articulate a version of what is typically called 'anti-realism'. One sees Heidegger as a constitutionalist or linguistic idealist who

radically breaks with or turns away from what had been previously advanced in the earlier work. The other reads the
later Heidegger as continuing the innovations of *Being and
Time* by further developing and deepening its investigation
of language. Our task is not necessarily to decide which
one of these two interpretations is correct or to endorse the
efforts of one in opposition to the other. Instead, what matters for our purposes is the way that both interpretations
formulate an understanding of media that effectively alters
the rules of the game.

Read from the perspective of linguistic constitutionalism
(as in the commentaries of Guignon, Taylor, Lafont and
others), Heidegger's argument has three key consequences
for how we approach and understand media.

1 Idealism

Heidegger's efforts deliberately overturn common-sense
realism, whereby it is assumed that there is a real world
of actual existing things that are then represented, more
or less adequately, in various mediated forms. 'Words and
language,' Heidegger asserts, 'are not just shells into which
things are packed for spoken and written inter-course. In the
word, in language, things first come to be and are' (ITM:
15). Understood in this way, the world of things, people and
events are not first out there and then subsequently represented by language and other forms of media. Instead, the
world that is assumed to be out there – the things, people
and events that comprise our shared sense of reality – is
always and already brought forth, structured and an effect of
language. This brings up an important question that is fundamental to both Media Studies and modern epistemology,
namely 'Do things exist outside our mediated experience of
them?' This question, the question of the reality or being

of the thing – the Thing itself, beyond and in excess of it becoming an object of mediation – is something (no pun intended) that increasingly comes to occupy Heidegger (and is explicitly investigated in chapter 3).

This particular formulation, it should also be noted, resonates with the concept of autopoiesis as it comes to be developed in second-order cybernetics and the work of Humberto Maturana and Francisco Varela (1980). 'To speak of an objectively existing world is misleading,' N. Katherine Hayles (1999: 136) writes, 'for the very idea of a world implies a realm that pre-exists its construction by an observer. Certainly there is something "out there," which for lack of a better term we can call "reality." But it comes into existence for us, and for all living creatures, *only through interactive processes determined solely by the organism's own organization*' (emphasis in the original). Although Heidegger found cybernetics (which he was only able to know in its initial form as articulated by its progenitor, Norbert Wiener) to be a kind of second-order metaphysics (OGS: 59), the term 'autopoiesis' is significant because it is related, quite literally in fact, to how Heidegger understands the poetic in its original, etymological sense, as poiesis – 'making' or 'bringing forth'. As Heidegger writes, quoting the words of the German poet Hölderlin, 'poetically man dwells' (PMD: 213).

2 Multiple realities

Different kinds of mediated representations, different 'organizational complexes' to use cybernetic terminology, produce and provide access to entirely different realities. Maps, for instance, do not simply represent different aspects of a particular existing territory. Instead, 'different maps,' as Carey (1989: 28) explains, 'bring the same environment alive in different ways; they produce quite different realities. Therefore, to live within the purview of different maps is to live within different realities.' Although the politically conservative Fox News and its liberal counter-weight MSNBC might cover the same event, like a debate between US presidential candidates, the picture of the world that each provides is often very different, such that viewers of one network occupy what seems to be an entirely different reality than viewers of the other.

Consequently real struggle – struggle over the very nature of reality itself – is something that takes place and transpires in media. Media shape the realities we occupy and are not just secondary reflections or shadows of some immediate world 'out there'. This means that the capability to create and deploy media is not simply about fashioning different and competing pictures of the world but constitutes a different world altogether. 'With the word "picture,"' Heidegger writes in the essay 'The Age of the World Picture' (which we will deal with in greater detail in chapter 4), 'we think first of all of a copy of something. Accordingly, the world picture would be a painting, so to speak, of what is as a whole. But "world picture" means more than this. We mean by it the world itself, the world as such . . .' (AWP: 129). Media, on this account, are not just pictures or copies of a pre-existing world but the means of picturing a world and exercising real power over the reality of this world itself.

3 Theory of truth

A constitutive approach to the understanding of language has important and inescapable consequences for the concept and theory of truth (a key theme of the next chapter). Typically we evaluate and judge the truthfulness of a statement or other form of mediated representation, like a news report, Facebook post or Twitter feed of some event in the world, by asking the questions Plato had formulated in the final book of *The Republic* – whether and to what extent the information provided in the report corresponds to the real thing or actual state of affairs. This is precisely what users of the internet, for example, want to know with articles provided by Wikipedia. Because an entry in this open-access encyclopaedia can be altered by anyone – those who are in the know as well as those who are not – critical users of this online resource are advised to check the information to make sure that it is accurate and that it is in fact a good and trustworthy representation of things. If, however, reality is originally constructed by mediated images, the question of truth can no longer be formulated as one of adequate correspondence between the description of things and the immediate reality itself. Instead, the question of truth will be otherwise – whether and to what extent things adequately correspond to representations. This complex of philosophical concepts, which involves things, truth and technology (specifically the techniques and technologies of representation) characterize the thematic elements that will be taken up and further investigated in the subsequent chapters. What is important at this particular juncture is that we recognize how these concepts come to be mediated in language by following Heidegger's confrontation with and thinking about language.

If we follow the interpretation of Heidegger's approach to language provided by Wrathall, we get a conceptualization of media that is able to contest the assumptions of realism without necessarily resorting to a form of linguistic idealism. Read in this fashion, Heidegger, as he had done since the time of *Being and Time*, begins by affirming the average everyday understanding of things. Ordinarily, the means of communication, whether spoken language or other forms of human expression, are considered to be tools or instruments that we have at our disposal to make representations of things or to externalize our thoughts. This ordinary understanding, Heidegger emphasizes and affirms, is not incorrect; it is just insufficient and incomplete. There is also, he argues, a more originary aspect to language whereby things first come to be disclosed and made available as such. As Terry Eagleton (2003: 55) explains, 'Language for Heidegger is not a mere instrument of communication, a secondary device for expressing "ideas": it is the very dimension in which human life moves, that which brings the world to be in the first place. Only where there is language is there "world", in the distinctively human sense.' This alternative form of anti-realism, as one might be tempted to call it, has, in its turn, at least three important consequences for the way we understand language and conceptualize media.

1 The question concerning technology

The language-as-tool formulation facilitates the accommodation of ordinary language to technology, specifically a characterization of technology that Heidegger describes as 'instrumental and anthropological' (QCT: 5). Understood in this fashion, language is considered to be a means to an end, or a medium. For Heidegger, then, there is a fundamental connection between ordinary language and the instrumental view of technology and media. This 'technological language', as Heidegger calls it in a 1962 lecture (TL: 129), achieves its end – this word understood, following Heidegger (EOP), as both 'completion' and 'fulfilment' – in cybernetics, the general science of control and communication (Wiener 1961). According to Heidegger, cybernetics not only reduces language to communication but also reduces communication to information transmission – an entirely calculable process that is perhaps better executed by machines than human organisms:

A machine carries out the technological process of feed-
back, which is marked by a regulator circuit just as well as
the report system of human language – if not in a technologically superior way. That is why the last step, if not
indeed the first, in all technological theories of language
is to explain 'that language is not an exclusive attribute of
man, but is one he may share to a certain degree with the
machines he has constructed' (Wiener 1950: 85). Such a
sentence is possible under the presupposition that what is
peculiar to language is reduced to, i.e. atrophied into, the
mere transmission, the reporting, of signals. (TL: 141)

This technological theory which regards language as a
neutral medium of communication, message transfer and
information transmission, limits, by the very assumption of
neutrality, critical investigations into whatever is made possible and normative by this particular way of overlooking the
mediation of things. Although barely mentioned in the text
of *Being and Time*, this pervasive technologicalization will
constitute one of the central issues of the later Heidegger
and we will return to it, in various ways, in the next three
chapters.

2 The language of poetry

Although language, in its ordinary aspect, is correlative
with information theory and an instrumental definition
of technology, it is not necessarily limited to this particular framework or paradigm. As Heidegger (TL: 142) points
out, again in the 1962 lecture, we can perceive 'behind all
technological transformations of the essence of language'
the remnants of a 'traditional language', a language that 'is
the preservation of what is original'. Consequently, it is possible to reconfigure and repurpose the technologized tools

of ordinary language in order to rediscover or to gesture in the direction of originary language. And for Heidegger (TL: 142), 'this is the task of the poet'. What distinguishes poetry, for Heidegger at least, is not the depth of its insight. It is not the case that poets have some unique and profound vision of things that is, for whatever reason, inaccessible to others (i.e. philosophers, scientists, theorists, etc.) and only able to be represented in verse. Instead, what interests Heidegger is poetry's radical superficiality. Poetry matters because of the way in which it engages with the material and materiality of ordinary language and how, in the process, it is able to break through, open up or otherwise gesture in the direction of the essential, originary dimension of language. Poetry, therefore, is Heidegger's model for what would constitute a responsible response, in the material of ordinary language, to what had been originally said in and by the *logos*. Although poetry, for Heidegger at least, is something experienced as words on the page, there is nothing to prevent us from extending his analysis and interpreting this term broadly to include other kinds of poetic work in music, experimental film, video art, digital media art, computer games, etc. Heidegger's thinking invites us to pursue these possibilities.

3 Rethinking truth

This alternative interpretation of language also has a transformative effect on the question of truth. But unlike linguistic constitutionalism, which simply reverses the usual procedure and replaces common-sense realism with a brand of idealism, truth will need to be fundamentally reconfigured. Because language is originally disclosing or revealing, 'truth' can no longer be conceptualized as a matter of measuring the correspondence between things and the representations of things. It is, in other words, not a matter of evaluating how well a statement about something represents the actual thing (realism) or how well something incorporates its symbolic construction (linguistic idealism). Instead, truth will need to be reconfigured as a matter of the revealing of what is. 'Language,' Eagleton (2003: 55) explains, 'always pre-exists the individual subject, as the very realm in which he or she unfolds; and it contains "truth" less in the sense that it is an instrument for exchanging accurate information than in the sense that it is the place where reality "un-conceals" itself, gives itself up to our contemplation.' This way of thinking introduces and mobilizes an anti-realist theory of truth that is not reducible to just another garden-variety idealism or constructivism. More specifically for our purposes, it raises a series of profound questions with which to address the status of mediated representations that, whilst technically correct (i.e. 'The camera never lies'), are nevertheless deeply problematic according to the unique Heideggerian approach to the thinking of truth that we take up and investigate in the next chapter.

CONCLUSION: THE REALITY OF MEDIA

Despite important transformations in his own research programme and approach, language was and continued to be a crucial issue for Heidegger, early and late, even if it is difficult to articulate his definitive view of the matter. On the one hand, what he has to say about language is not univocal or entirely consistent. Heidegger's understanding of language, then, is not static; it evolves and develops over the course of his career. And to make matters worse, his own language, the very words he uses to talk about this, also change and do not remain fixed. Language turns out to be a dynamic, moving target. On the other hand, interpretations of the later Heidegger – where language increasingly comes to take centre-stage and his own writing becomes involved, in both form and content, with poetry – vary significantly. Consequently, the later Heidegger has been read as supporting either a revolutionary brand of linguistic constitutionalism or an anti-realist position that contests and does not resolve into mere idealism.

So where does this leave things? Let us conclude by making three general comments that will be important for the chapters that follow.

1 There is no-thing outside media

If language (the 'first' media in terms of both temporal sequence and status) is originally revealing and the way entities comes to be disclosed in their being, then whatever comes to be, whatever has existence and is considered some-thing, is only in and by the mediation of language. Conversely, whatever remains in excess or outside language will have been, quite literally, no-thing. As Heidegger (NOL: 62–3) explains in an essay entitled 'The Nature of Language':

> Only where the word for the thing has been found is the thing a thing. Only thus is it. Accordingly we must stress as follows: no thing is where the word, that is, the name, is lacking. The word alone gives being to the thing ... Something is only where the appropriate and therefore competent word names a thing as being, and so establishes the given being as a being. (NOL: 62–3)

This is, as we have seen at the beginning of the chapter, an insight perhaps best articulated by Derrida's controversial statement: *il n'y a pas de hors-texte*. But it is for our purposes perhaps best stated in an even more generalizable form: 'There is nothing outside media.'

2 *Recursive remediation*

Since there is no-thing outside language, there is also no possibility of 'stepping outside language'. We cannot, in other words, formulate or occupy some meta-linguistic position that could then be used as a platform to reflect on and say something about language outside and in excess of language.[5] Everything is already caught up in and unable to escape from this linguistic enclosure. Or as Adilkno describes it in the epigraph to this chapter, to say something about media is always and already to be involved in media. This is, it is important to remember, not necessarily a problem of 'circular reasoning' and it is Heidegger, in particular, who helps us think it through.

At the beginning of *Being and Time*, Heidegger notes how the very means of the investigation is itself caught up in what is investigated. This is not some unique or singular problem. It is, as Briankle Chang (1996: ix–x) points out, 'the epistemic quandary of writers from diverse fields (such as philosophy of mind, philosophy of language, cultural anthropology) in which the act of the investigation is implicated in the object of inquiry as its condition of possibility.' In these situations, 'what is decisive,' Heidegger (BT: 195) explains, 'is not to get out of the circle but to come into it in the right way.' Entering the circle in the right way entails, first and foremost, that we recognize how our efforts are always situated *in medias res*, in the middle of things, and that the assumed and privileged position of immediacy – some kind of extra-medial or meta-linguistic point of view – is a fiction.

This means, on the one hand, that there is no escaping media. But this insight does not necessarily result in nihilism or even narcissism. It simply means that Media Studies needs to be conceptualized as a self-reflective endeavour that works within media in order to say something about media. This

recursive effort has been identified with the term 'remediation' by Jay David Bolter and Richard Grusin (2000),
who explicitly recognize, following the insights of Marshall
McLuhan (1995), who in turn developed his ideas following the groundbreaking work of Harold Innis (1951), that
the content of any medium is always and only another form
of media. On the other hand, it means that Media Studies
is and must be pursued as a self-reflexive science. It can, in
other words, no longer simply endorse the pretensions of
naive realism nor conceive of its efforts as a matter of evaluating the correctness of mediated representations to the way
things really are. Media Studies will have been a speculative
science . . . or not at all.

3 Anti-realism

Whether we read Heidegger as a strict constitutionalist,
that is, someone who believes that the reality of our world
is something constituted, construed or constructed by the
words, symbols and other forms of media that we deploy,
or whether we interpret his work as staking out a claim to a
position that is considerably less idealistic, what is certain is
that Heidegger contests, interrupts and significantly reconfigures the standard operating presumptions of realism. This
is a real game-changer for media and Media Studies. Whilst
realism and a particular Platonic understanding of representation has gone largely unchallenged and been left virtually
unquestioned for millennia, in contesting the assumptions
of realism, Heidegger not only breaks with Plato and the
metaphysical tradition that develops in his wake but also
problematizes the traditional concept of truth – truth as
correctness, correspondence, fidelity and verification – as
it has been mobilized in modern science. Once we give up
the ghost of realism, all bets are off. Everything needs to be

rethought, not the least of which is, what do we mean by truth? What is a Thing? And, thereafter, what sort of truthful thing is the media? These are the topics of the subsequent chapters.

2

MEDIATED TRUTH

INTRODUCTION: THE TRUE, THE CORRECT AND THE STOLEN WHEELBARROW

> Unconcealment in accordance with which nature pre-
> sents itself as a *calculable complex* of the effects of forces can
> indeed permit *correct determinations*; but precisely through
> these successes the danger can remain that in the midst of
> all that is correct the true will withdraw.
>
> QCT: 26

It is ironic that, despite (or perhaps because of) the central
role played by truth in Heidegger's work, his philosophical
analysis of technology has so often been misinterpreted and
misrepresented. For a thinker frequently accused of using
impenetrable prose, the above quotation encapsulates with
admirable clarity and succinctness the importance truth plays
for Heidegger in specific relation to technology (a specificity we then further extend to our particular focus on media

technology). This quotation contains two related issues that are particularly relevant to the contemporary mediascape:

1. The conceptual distinction between what may be *correct* and what is ultimately *true*. This distinction is readily apparent in computer-generated imagery, or CGI, now something of a standard feature of the Hollywood blockbuster film. CGI is able to produce impressive and believable images of, for example, giant robots ravaging the streets of a major US city. Correct in the sense that they are entirely convincing, these depictions are nevertheless fabrications and fictions generated by a computer simulation. Historically, the difference between reality and such imaginative fabrications was clear. Apart from clever tricks like *trompe l'oeil* paintings, the two were seldom confused. Today, the distinction is much less apparent, and, although frequently misrepresented as an endorser of fakeness, Baudrillard's concept of *simulation* (1984) describes the complex imbrication of the real with its representations to the extent that they can no longer be easily separated.

2. The consequently derived paradox whereby the truth becomes hidden, not because of efforts to cover it up, but paradoxically, because it is displaced by an over-abundance of correctness. In *The Mass Ornament*, Siegfried Kracauer encapsulates this insight with his observation that: 'In the illustrated magazines, people see the very world that the illustrated magazines prevent them from perceiving' (1995 [1963]: 58). A more recent illustration is provided by Reality TV and the way its excessively explicit content (ironically) conceals the very reality it purports to expose and reveal.

In the context of the mediation, representation and technological framing of things, taking both points together enables us to recognize the usually unacknowledged ways in which truth is routinely subordinated to correctness. Working systematically through the excerpt, we can see how '*unconcealment in accordance with which nature presents itself as a calculable complex of the effects of forces*' expresses the manner in which, in our techno-scientific era, we tend to see the world around us as an innately measurable interrelationship of causes and effects – the calculable complex. When we explicitly consider and describe these causes and effects, we undeniably produce a series of 'correct determinations'. However, accurate as they may be, such determinations still lack something that goes beyond what Heidegger pointedly terms elsewhere the '*merely* correct' (QCT: 6). With the 'mere' use of the word 'merely', Heidegger deftly conveys the counter-intuitive force of this philosophical insight. He identifies a problem that has been over 2,500 years in the making – the unreflexive manner in which we are preconditioned to equate truth with correctness.

In contemporary media culture this preconditioning occurs in an unprecedentedly natural and systematic fashion with profound ideological consequences. It is not just that a philosophical distinction can be made between truth and correctness (point 1) but that this distinction is simultaneously exacerbated *and* obfuscated in the very mediated processes by which correct, but not necessarily true, determinations are made (point 2). Put more simply, and to repeat, it is in the very guise of being so explicit that the media manages to conceal its true impact. Heidegger's seemingly abstract philosophical distinction, therefore, has very practical implications for our actual lived experience within an increasingly technological mediascape. It informs, for instance, critical theories of media that seek to go beyond face-value understandings of representation that are based on what we shall shortly see is an inadequately interrogated correspondence theory of truth. Consequently, the often uncritical, unreflexive and excessively optimistic belief that new forms of interactivity are unproblematically empowering fails to see that 'perhaps the most important time to worry about the workings of power is when we're told that it is no longer a concern because we're all empowered by the advent of interactive media technologies' (Andrejevic 2009: 48).

It is, in this context, hard to improve upon Marshall McLuhan's previously cited formula: 'The medium is the message.' From a Heideggerian perspective, this aphorism works as a highly succinct expression of truth's displacement by correctness. For example, in the case of the widespread valorization of digital technology, the medium has indeed become the message, as 'interactivity' has largely become an end in itself, an end from which qualitiative considerations are largely absent. Susan Sontag illustrates this point in relation to the earlier technology of photography:

> This very passivity – and ubiquity – of the photographic record is photography's 'message', its aggression . . . There is an aggression implicit in every use of the camera. This is as evident in the 1840s and 1850s, photography's glorious first two decades, as in all the succeeding decades during which technology made possible an ever increasing spread of that mentality which looks at the world as a set of potential photographs . . . The subsequent industrialization of camera technology only carried out a promise inherent in photography from its very beginning: to democratize all experiences by translating them into images. (Sontag 1979: 7)

More recently, Slavoj Žižek describes how western media excel at facilitating a form of ideological bluff – an ideological effect is achieved in the very guise of superficially 'non-ideological' media content. Heidegger's truth/correctness distinction, therefore, helps us catch things designed to pass right under our noses,[1] thereby avoiding the mistake, recounted by Žižek on more than one occasion, of the security guard who suspects a factory worker of stealing: 'Every evening, as he leaves the factory, the wheelbarrow he rolls in front of him is carefully inspected. The guards can find nothing. It is always empty. Finally, the penny drops: what the worker is stealing are the wheelbarrows themselves' (2008: 1). Heidegger's insight that it is *precisely through these successes* [that] *the true will withdraw* (point 2) thus continues to have profound importance for our understanding of media.

PLATO'S CAVE: CORRESPONDENCE AS THE DEFAULT SETTING

Next compare our nature in respect of education and its lack to such an experience as this. Picture men dwelling in a sort of subterranean cavern with a long entrance open to the light on its entire width. Conceive of them as having their legs and necks fettered from childhood, so that they remain in the same spot, able to look forward only, and prevented by the fetters from turning their heads. Picture further the light from a fire burning higher up and at a distance behind them, and between the fire and the prisoners and above them a road along which a low wall has been built, as the exhibitors of puppet-shows have partitions before the men themselves, above which they show the puppets.

Plato 1987: 514a–b

According to Heidegger (PDT and BAT), the crucial difference between *truth* and *correctness* is both revealed and subsequently effaced in one of the pivotal texts of the western philosophical tradition, Plato's 'Allegory of the Cave'. Originally written around 380 BCE and recounted at the beginning of book VII of *Republic*, the allegory depicts a movie theatre *avant la lettre*. As described by Socrates, the cave dwellers operate as if everything that appears on the wall (prototypical cinema or monitor screen) is in fact real. They bestow names on the different shadows that are projected on the wall, devise clever methods to predict their sequence and behaviour, and hand out awards to each other for demonstrated proficiency in knowing such things (Plato 1987: 515a–b).

At a crucial turning point in the story, one of the captives is released. Unbound by some ambiguous external action, he is compelled to look at the source of the shadows – small puppets paraded in front of a large fire. Although standing up for the first time and looking at the light that provides illumination for the shadow images is initially painful and disorienting, the prisoner eventually comes to understand 'that what he had seen before was all a cheat and an illusion' (Plato 1987: 515d). In this way, the former prisoner comes to see that what he and his colleagues had previously asserted about their world does not, in fact, agree with what he now perceives. Understood in this way, the allegory narrates, Heidegger argues, a sequence of events whereby the prisoner's gaze 'becomes more correct' and truth becomes characterized as ὀρθότης – the 'correctness of representation' to the thing represented (PDT: 177).

This particular understanding of truth – truth as correct agreement or correspondence – has dominated the history of western thought and its seminal works. It is, for example, evident in:

- Aristotle's *De interpretatione* in which: 'the soul's "experiences," its νοήματα ('representations'), are likenings of things' (BT: 257);
- the scholastic definition of truth as *adaequatio intellectus et rei*, the adequation of thought to things (BT: 257);
- René Descartes's claim that 'the word "truth", in the strict

sense, denotes the conformity of thought with its object' (Descartes 1991 [1983]: 139);
- Immanuel Kant's *Critique of Pure Reason*, which grants, without any critical hesitation whatsoever (a somewhat ironic gesture in a book that is all about 'critique'), that truth is 'the agreement of knowledge with its object' (Kant 1965 [1956]: 97).

This formulation of truth sounds perfectly reasonable. As Heidegger explains in a lecture course from 1937–8, 'the determination of truth as correctness, together with its counterpart, namely incorrectness (falsity), is in fact clear as day. Because this conception of truth emerges, as is obvious, entirely from the natural way of thinking, and corresponds to it, it has lasted throughout the centuries and has long ago been hardened into something taken for granted' (BQP: 15–16). In other (unavoidably tautologous) words, this formulation of truth seems to be true. Known as the 'correspondence theory of truth' (as the term straightforwardly suggests), truth understood as the correctness of representation to the thing represented seems to correspond exactly to what we typically understand and experience as truth.

In a similar fashion, Communication Studies and investigations of media privilege various categories of the correct – accuracy, fidelity, validity, credibility, etc. – and formulate enquires like:

- How does one know whether the information presented on a web page, contained in a *Wikipedia* article or posted on a blog is in fact trustworthy or credible?
- How can we be certain that a Hollywood film or television docu-drama that is 'based on a true story' gets it right, tells the entire story as it is and does not embellish things for cheap dramatic thrills?

- How can we trust that the other with whom we interact in an online chat, through email or by way of a social network like Facebook is in fact telling the truth about his/her identity?
- How can we be sure that the information that comes to us through news outlets like the *New York Times*, Al Jazeera and the BBC is in fact an accurate and objective report of real-world events?

In all of these situations and enquiries, the missing Heideggerian question is what is meant by a 'truth' that goes beyond the merely correct? From Heidegger's radically different perspective, the fundamental question is not, for example, whether the person you are chatting with is who they say they are, or even whether online chat constitutes a true form of communication at all? 'A true form of communication' in these conventional senses is just another way of saying 'a more correct form of communication.' What Heidegger seeks to highlight and thereafter problematize is the understanding of truth that is already operationalized by this very question.

Consequently, Heidegger's question is more fundamental and ontological. He asks what do we have in mind when we ask whether something is true? What is true, and what is truth? This is precisely because *truth*, as Heidegger explains, is not just one issue among others. It is *the* defining question of philosophy, which has, from at least the time of Aristotle, been explicitly characterized as 'the Science of truth' (BT: 256). In addressing the heady question 'what is truth?', Heidegger not only does some impressive and groundbreaking philosophical analysis but provides an innovative approach to this matter that can help us understand the complexity of media representations, the accuracy of information and the task of critical media production and consumption.

THE QUESTION OF TRUTH

There are three theses which characterize the way in which the essence of truth has been traditionally taken and the way it is supposed to have been first defined: 1) that the 'locus' of truth is assertion (judgment); 2) that the essence of truth lies in the 'agreement' of the judgment with its object; 3) that Aristotle, the father of logic, not only assigned truth to judgment as its primordial locus but has set going the definition of 'truth' as 'agreement'.

BT: 257

The question of truth occupies a central position in Heidegger's *magnum opus*, *Being and Time* – quite literally since the investigation of this matter is situated at the exact centre of the work and serves as the point of transition from the first to the second main division. According to Heidegger's explanation, *truth* is not something that is 'out there' to be discovered in things but is essentially a relative concept. It subsists in the agreement or *correspondence* between a statement about something, what is commonly called a 'judgement', and the object about which the statement is made. Heidegger illustrates this with a rather simple example: someone with his back turned to a wall claims that a picture on the wall is hanging askew. The truth of the man's statement, namely that the picture is not positioned correctly on the wall, can be easily evaluated by having him turn around and compare the content of his statement to the actual thing. If the statement does in fact agree with or correspond to the actual situation of the object, then it is true; if not, it is considered false.

This formulation seems to describe perfectly the situation regarding media content and representation. When we are, for example, confronted with the report of some event, the accuracy or truthfulness of the account is typically evaluated by comparing what is asserted in the report with what really happened. This is probably best illustrated not in situations of truth, where there is agreement, but in circumstances where the opposite occurs, where the report or assertion is found to be inaccurate or where something has been falsified or misrepresented. In the run-up to the second Iraq war in March 2003, for instance, then US president George W. Bush and his administration issued a number of ominous statements regarding Iraq's development, possession and potential use of weapons of mass destruction (WMD). News of these statements, which consisted of various official documents, press briefings, public speeches and hearings before national legislatures and international organizations like the United Nations, circulated in both US and UK media, and they presented the public with an image of Iraq as a rogue nation with the capabilities to cause immeasurable harm to its own people and other countries in the region. The *truth* of these news reports and other media assertions was eventually tested and demonstrated during the invasion and subsequent occupation of Iraq. Although the expectation was that the invading forces would, at some point, turn up stockpiles of weapons or at least facilities for their manufacture, nothing like this was ever discovered. There were, in fact, no stockpiles of chemical and biological weapons. Consequently, the assertion that Iraq either had these weapons or was in the process of developing such weapons turned out to be inaccurate and false. The actual state of affairs, the real situation on the ground in Iraq, did not correspond to the various media assertions that had been made concerning WMDs.

Another instance of this can found in the less sober realm of entertainment. Popular game shows during the 'golden age of television' often used a format based upon a final revelation. Two of these were *To Tell the Truth* (USA,

1956–2002) and *Call My Bluff* (UK, 1965–1988 and 1996–
2005). *To Tell the Truth* featured a panel of four celebrities
who were confronted by a group of three individuals, each
of whom claimed to be a particular individual who had some
unusual background, notable life experience or unique occupation. The celebrity panel was charged with interrogating
the three candidates and, based on the responses to their
questions, decided which one of the three was actually the
person s/he purported to be. In essence, they had to determine which one was telling the truth. In this exchange, two
of the contestants engaged in deliberate deception, answering the questions of the celebrity panel by pretending to be
someone they were not, while the remaining contestant told
the truth. The 'moment of truth' came at the game's conclusion, when the programme's host asked the pivotal question
'Will the real so-and-so please stand up?', upon which one
of the three stood. In doing so, this one individual demonstrated that s/he had been telling the truth, while the other
two had engaged in deliberate and calculated deception
(Gunkel 2011). *Call My Bluff* involved a similar basic prem-
ise but, instead of a mystery guest, it involved two teams of
three personalities who each read out the definition of an
esoteric word or phrase for the opposing team to attempt to
guess the true/correct answer. These game shows were based
on and played with every aspect of what Heidegger describes
as the 'correspondence theory of truth'.

This formula has recently evolved into more sophisticated
forms like the new docu-dramas *The Secret Millionaire* and
Undercover Boss. Here, the dramatic revelation found at the
programme's conclusion (reality TV's version of pornography's 'money shot'; see Taylor and Harris 2008: 158 and
170) is also present but its anticipation is supplemented by
an ongoing narrative jeopardy: will the undercover philan-
thropist/boss be rumbled before they can reveal their 'true'

nature and bestow their largesse? These formats demonstrate new manifestations of the naturalized (unquestioned)
characterization of truth as correctness. The secret guarded
so closely by the millionaires/bosses is undoubtedly a correct
one (viewers know that, despite the short-term masquerade as
an unpaid volunteer/co-worker, these figures are in fact rich
CEOs and managers) but fails to reveal (in Heidegger's par-
lance *unconceal*) other, perhaps more uncomfortable, truths
that are disclosed during the programme. For example, the
causes of, and potential solutions for, the great social inequal-
ity that provides the show with its essential viewability remain
largely unacknowledged and undisclosed. Most significantly,
at the end of each episode, there is no dwelling upon the
explicit mismatch between the poverty and wealth so clearly
and emotionally portrayed. Instead, the programme ends
with a reassuring sense of correspondence as the eponymous
millionaires return to their suitably luxurious homes.

THE PROBLEM WITH THE REAL THING

The conception of truth as correctness of representation is
taken for granted everywhere, in philosophy just as in extra-
philosophical opinion.

BQP: 17

The correspondence theory of truth seems so obviously true
that, as Heidegger points out, it dominates both philosophical and non-philosophical modes of thought. It is precisely
this apparently widespread and unquestioned assumption,
this 'being taken for granted everywhere', however, that
is, for Heidegger, precisely the problem. He thus submits
correspondence theory to critical questioning, producing a meticulous investigation and analysis that identifies
important aspects that he claims have gone virtually unno-

ticed for over two thousand years (BT: 259). Whether this is an immodest claim or not, it is clear that Heidegger has a unique gift for identifying everyday common-sense and taken-for-granted ways of thinking and then submitting these to an exhaustive (and some might even say an 'exhausting') analysis to investigate their origins, operations and consequences. This is a particularly useful mode of questioning with which to address what the media takes for granted, or, to use Roland Barthes's (1973 [1957]) shorthand phrase, 'what goes without saying'.

In *Being and Time*, Heidegger's investigation of this matter proceeds by further developing the previous example of a man with his back to the wall making assertions about a picture hanging askew. In order to measure or evaluate the extent to which a particular statement or representation corresponds to the actual state of affairs, one must, as Heidegger indicates, have unmitigated and direct access to the Real thing. When the individual who claims that the 'picture on the wall is askew' wishes to know whether this statement is 'true' or 'false', this can only be discovered and demonstrated by 'turning around' and looking at the 'Real picture', or the 'Thing itself that is' (BT: 260). As in the case of *To Tell the Truth*, *Call My Bluff* or *The Secret Millionaire*, at some point the real thing has to be made to stand up and show itself as such.

Access to this 'real thing' can be provided in one of two ways. On the one hand, the real may be revealed in advance, or what philosophers call a priori. This is the situation that is typically operative with social networking applications like Facebook and Google. Since users of these communication technologies, as Lisa Nakamura (2007: 49) points out, 'already know the identities of their interlocutors', they are able to evaluate whether their friend's avatar, a Facebook profile or a screen name and description, is an accurate representation of the real person or not. On the other hand, access to the 'real thing' can be situated after the fact, or a posteriori. In this situation, the real is made available and exposed as such only after a considerable engagement with its mediated representations. This is the experience commonly reported by internet users who initiate contact online and then endeavour to meet each other face to face (F2F) in real life (RL). The outcome of such RL meetings is either pleasantly surprising, as one comes to realize that the real person is pretty much what one had expected, or terribly disturbing, as it becomes clear that the 'real thing' is nothing like he or she pretended to be (Figure 2.1). The former, pleasant outcome is evident, for example, in the marketing campaigns of next-gen computer-dating services like e-Harmony.com and Match.com, where users connect with their one true love. The latter and much more disturbing possibility has

Figure 2.1　Chat rooms: the awful truth

gained considerable prominence in press coverage of police
sting operations, where law enforcement agents, posing as
underage minors online, arrange RL rendezvous with sexual
predators, scam artists and paedophiles.

This is, then, the way we typically understand and evaluate truth. What is needed, and what is indispensable for a
demonstration of truth, is access to the real thing as it really
is. The problem, of course, is that this kind of direct and
immediate access to the real thing is often difficult, if not
impossible, to achieve. Let's return to Heidegger's example
of someone who makes a statement about a picture. Is this
statement about truth true? Does it, according to the standard that it articulates, agree with its object? If the reader
of Heidegger's text, in which this assertion is made, turns
around, can she demonstrate the adequacy of the statement
by actually perceiving someone with his back to the wall
making statements about pictures that are hanging askew?
Perhaps this reading is too literal. It may be the case that
Heidegger's statement is not necessarily about an actual 'real
event' but is the representation of a common experience that
we can easily imagine – an idea as opposed to a real situation. In that case, however, the statement in the text would
be demonstrated by comparing it to another kind of statement made elsewhere by the reader. Asking these questions
appears to lead one in circles, in which every statement about
something is compared to other statements and representations and not necessarily to the immediate perception of the
real thing.

Consequently, in all but the most trivial of circumstances,
when we, as Heidegger puts it, 'turn around' to evaluate the
truth of an assertion, we do not behold the real thing in its
unclothed nakedness but, rather, have to deal with another
set of assertions and representations. We are therefore limited to, and appear to be caught up in, a situation of recursive

mediation, like that characterized by Jay David Bolter in his investigation of words in a dictionary. Here, words are defined not by reference to real things but by reference to other words:

> The definition of any word, if pursued far enough through the dictionary, will lead you in circles. This paradox is the foundation of semiotics. A sign system is a set of rules for relating elements. The rules are arbitrary, and the system they generate is self-contained. There is no way to get 'outside' the system to the world represented, because, as in the dictionary, signs can only lead you elsewhere in the same system. (Bolter 1991: 197)

What the dictionary demonstrates is that our use of words is always and already restricted to the system of linguistic signifiers and never able to get outside language to ascertain the referent, the so-called 'real thing', or what semioticians call the 'transcendental signified'.

This apparent criticism is, as Heidegger points out, one of the standard objections and counter-examples to correspondence theory:

> To be sure, in the course of time objections arose against this conception of truth. These objections were based, specifically, on doubt as to whether our representations reached the being itself in itself at all and did not rather remain enclosed within the circuit of their own activity . . . Consequently knowledge and assertions consist in the representation of representations and hence in a combination of representations. (BQP: 16)

According to Heidegger, this 'doctrine' that representations relate only to other representations is called *idealism*, while 'the counter-claim, according to which our representations reach the things themselves . . . has been called *realism*' (BQP: 17). What is of particular interest for Heidegger, however, is not what makes idealism and realism different. Instead, what he finds noteworthy is what they already agree upon and share in order to articulate different opinions and occupy contrary positions. 'These hostile brothers,' Heidegger explains, 'are unwittingly in complete accord with regard to the essence, i.e. with regard to what provides the presupposition and the very possibility of their controversy: that the relation to beings is a representing of them and that the truth of the representation consists in its correctness' (BQP: 17). Paradoxically, it is what constitutes the *essence* of correctness that, in the very mode of the media's frequently excessively correct representations, remains most hidden.

SCREENING THE REAL: THE CORRESPONDENCE THEORY AND MEDIA

Has anyone been discussing the matter of how we can distinguish between what is true and what is false? . . . Those who speak enthusiastically of the great volume of statements about the world available on the Internet do not usually address how we may distinguish the true from the false.

Postman 2000: 92

Postman's question regarding the truth (or falsity) of statements made on the internet helps to illustrate the particular function played by the correspondence theory in media and the role media plays in structuring our understanding of the correspondence theory. Let us consider three examples:

1. We can see – or better hear – the correspondence theory at work in sound recording, whether that be on magnetic

Figure 2.2   The Victor Talking Machine Company trademark

tape, vinyl disc or MP3s. One of the most recognizable images concerning sound recording is the Victor Talking Machine Company's trademark, which depicts Nipper the dog sitting obediently before the horn of a gramophone, listening to a recording of 'his master's voice' (Figure 2.2). The message of the image is clear, the reproduced sound of this particular technological apparatus is so close in its correspondence to the real thing that the dog, the traditional pictorial symbol of fidelity in European portraiture (hence the common name 'Fido'), is unable to tell the difference. Despite this expectation, however, most recordings, especially in the networked digital age, do not simply copy or reproduce a real thing or 'live' event. In fact, the majority of recordings in popular music manufacture an ideal version of something that did not, in fact, ever take place as such – mixing together, for example, the performances of musicians who never occupied the same space and time or reversing the expected relationship between live performance and recording as in instances of lip-syncing (i.e. Whitney Houston at Super Bowl XXV in 1991 and Beyoncé at the second inaugural of US President Barak Obama in 2013). In these cases, the recording corresponds not to an actual live performance but to an ideal performance created in and by the technology of audio recording. The issue, however, is not whether the ultimate referent of the recording is a real, live performance or some idealized content. Either way, the fidelity or truthfulness of the recording is a matter of correspondence or the likening of one thing to another.

2. The rise of reality TV programmes like *Big Brother*, *Survivor* and *The Biggest Loser* demonstrates the way contemporary media have so successfully recalibrated our viewing habits to the correspondence theory of truth that it remains largely unacknowledged or even recognized as such. Reality TV's iconoclastic arrival as a radically new mode of media discourse lies in its unprecedented ability to deliver apparently correct representations of real events via its ubiquitous 'fly-on-the-wall' cameras. In this way, the genre bears out the notion that idealism and realism share a fraternal connection. Reality TV is realist to the extent that it is fixated upon the ability to represent all elements (no matter how mundane) of its objectified subjects' lives and their erstwhile intimate moments. It purports to represent what really happened in its immediacy. But it is also idealist to the extent that this apparent realism is, in fact, dominated by highly constrained and carefully stipulated formal practices that correspond not so much to real things and events as to various tropes and expectations that we now readily associate with media produced reality – i.e. the use of the (what used to be considered 'edgy' but is now almost standard) shaky handheld camera of *cinema-vérité*, the intimate video diaries that function like a postmodern version of the Catholic confessional and the

melodramatic narrative structures that turn everything into a
crisis, conflict or end-of-season cliffhanger.

3. Finally, there is internet content, specifically those
user-generated sources like Wikipedia that allow anyone
and everyone to post or edit information. The principal and persistent concern with Wikipedia, especially for
university teachers and students, has to do with truth and
truth specifically operationalized as correspondence. If one
enquires about the truthfulness of the information contained in a Wikipedia article, population statistics of the
African elephant for instance,[2] one usually questions whether
the statements provided in the article agree with and correspond to the actual state of affairs – the real number of
elephants in the world. One seeks, in the language used by
Heidegger, to 'turn around' in order to evaluate the accuracy
of the reported data to the Real thing as it actually is. In
the case of the population of African elephants, the truth or
falsity of the reported information would require that one
have access to and be able to make a realistic enumeration
of actually existing elephants, which is clearly something
very few individuals would ever be able to achieve for themselves. For this reason, the statements made in Wikipedia,
or any other media outlet for that matter, are not necessarily
evaluated against the real state of affairs. The requirements
for this kind of realism are typically impractical and less
than realistic. They are instead compared to other statements and representations provided elsewhere, usually in
some other venue or form of media, which is the procedure
Heidegger identifies with the term 'idealism'. In either case,
however, it is still a matter of comparing the information
that is asserted in the article to the population of African
elephants; it is still a matter of measuring the correctness
of representation to the being of this particular object. 'If
our representations and assertions,' Heidegger argues, 'are

supposed to conform to the object, then this being must be accessible in advance in order to present itself as a standard and measure for the conformity with it. In short, the being, in this case the thing, must be out in the open' (BQP: 18).

In these distinctly non-abstract, real-world examples, therefore, we can see how idealism and realism, despite their obvious differences, still endorse and operate according to an understanding of truth as correspondence or correctness of representation. Although they may disagree as to what this correspondence actually involves – other representations versus the things themselves – they both endorse and affirm that truth is essentially a matter of agreement. Heidegger, by contrast pursues the question of truth beyond this default setting.

BEYOND CORRESPONDENCE: THE MEDIA AS COMMUNICATIVELY DETERMINATIVE EXHIBITION

Once the truth of being becomes equated with the light of unchanging intelligibility, the nature of truth shifts to the ability of statements to reflect or refer reliably to entities. With the steadiness of propositional truth comes the tendency to relate to being as a type, a form, or an anticipated shape. With being as a steady form, entities gain their reality through their being typified. Already in Plato we see the seeds of the Western drive to standardize things, to find what is dependable and typical in them. Truth as the disclosure process, as the play of revealing/concealing disappears behind the scene in which the conscious mind grasps bright objects apprehended as clear, unwavering, rational forms. As humans develop the ability to typify and apprehend

formal realities, the loss of truth as emergent disclosure
goes unnoticed.

Heim 1993: 68

Our long cultural history of correspondence-based thinking
means that, whether it is a matter of evaluating the fidelity
of a popular recording or the trustworthiness of information that is reported in a Wikipedia article, truth is always
presumed to be a matter of measuring the correctness of
representation to the actual being of some object. Michael
Heim's description of the consequences of this reduction of
truth to correspondence helps to explain what gets lost or
covered up in the process. As Heidegger insightfully points
out, 'if our representations and assertions are supposed to
conform to the object, then this being must be accessible
in advance'; it must already be given and 'out in the open'
(BQP: 18).

In response to this problem, Heidegger advocates an
alternative conceptualization of truth that is not so much an
innovation as a return to a 'more original' and fundamental
understanding of the concept.

> Truth as correctness of representation presupposes, in order
> to be what it is (assimilation to the object), the openness of
> beings by which they become capable of being ob-jects in
> the first place and by which the representation becomes a
> faculty of presenting something before itself as such. This
> openness appeared consequently as the ground of the pos-
> sibility of correctness. Accordingly, correctness cannot
> constitute the original essence of truth if it itself is depend-
> ent on something more original. The original essence of
> truth must then be sought in a return to this openness.
> (BQP: 18)

In formulating this more original understanding of truth, Heidegger returns to and capitalizes upon the ancient Greek word for truth, ἀλήθεια [*aletheia*], which he translates as 'unconcealing', 'uncovering' or 'unhiddenness'. This translation is not incidental; it is crucial for understanding Heidegger's conceptual intervention. 'If,' Heidegger writes in the essay 'On the Essence of Truth', 'we translate ἀλήθεια as "unconcealment" rather than "truth," this translation is not merely more literal; it contains the directive to rethink the ordinary concept of truth in the sense of the correctness of statements and to think it back to that still uncomprehended disclosedness and disclosure of beings' (OET: 127). This subtle shift in emphasis makes all the difference. Unconcealing, Heidegger argues, is 'the fundamental trait of being itself' and, unlike the adequacy of a statement about something or the correctness of a representation to the thing represented, is not 'a characteristic of the knowing of beings' (PDT: 179).

What Heidegger advances, therefore, is not a new and competing viewpoint that would amount to another theory of truth but a retrieval of a more primordial definition that originally grounds and supports correspondence theory. 'Originally,' Heidegger argues, 'there resides in this determination of truth as unconcealedness nothing like correctness, but, instead, all correctness of assertion resides in the unconcealedness of beings. For the orientation of representations toward beings and their conformity with beings are possible only if beings dwell in unconcealedness' (BQP: 92). In other words, the correspondence theory of truth – whether one tends to endorse the idealist or realist version – is only able to be true on the basis of a prior disclosure of things (whereby things are first out in the open) that makes agreement or correspondence possible in the first place. In this way, then, Heidegger actually *performs* this alternative characterization of truth in the course of presenting it; he uncovers truth as (originally) uncovering.

The direct implication of this for media is that, if truth is not originally a matter of the adequacy of representation (that is, the likening of one thing to another), then the status and function of any form of media assertion whether in spoken discourse, writing, printing, painting, photography, television, web sites, video games, and so on will also need to be situated otherwise. Accordingly, the truth of a representation is not, as it is customarily assumed to be, a matter of the agreement of an assertion (i.e. 'the picture on the wall is hanging askew') to the object or state of affairs about which the assertion is made. Instead, assertion constitutes a *'communicatively determinative exhibition'* (BPP: 210) whereby the being of something comes to be plucked out of its undifferentiated entanglement in its environment and exhibited as such. It is, as Heidegger argues, the process of uncovering entities so that they can be seen in their uncoveredness (BT: 262). Carey, following Heidegger, locates this revealing or uncovering of being in λογος [*logos*]. It is not the case, he argues, that there are first things in the world 'out there' and then words that we subsequently use to refer to and talk about these things. The order of precedence is reversed. Whatever is 'out there' comes into being in and by being spoken (about). This does not, however, mean that the world is somehow a fiction created by language. Neither Carey nor Heidegger would endorse this extreme form of social constructivism. Rather, Heidegger encourages us to think of language as 'the house of Being', that is, the means by which Being is uncovered and disclosed to us. This is precisely what Wrathall (2011: 155) had sought to identify with the term 'originary language' (see chapter 1).

A practical example of this can be seen in the case of Newtonian physics. Heidegger argues that, prior to the assertions made by Sir Isaac Newton, what we now know as Newton's laws, were neither true nor false. This is not because the entities (i.e. bodies and forces) that are described by these assertions did not exist in the world. It is because they did not show themselves in this particular way, that is, as bodies and forces, until Newton's theorizing framed and exhibited them as such (BT: 269). This is obviously highly relevant to the role played by the media (as indicated by the now well-established discipline of media framing research) – by their very nature they frame and exhibit our various acts of communication to the extent, that like Newtonian physics, it becomes difficult to think at all without such framing being taken as an already given factor in our experience. This concept of the mediated frame and of framing will, for Heidegger in particular, be directly connected to the question concerning technology. In fact, for Heidegger, it is en-framing [*Gestell*] that constitutes the essence of technology (see chapter 4).

SPEAKING OF REPRESENTATION: UNCONCEALMENT

The basic achievement of speech consists in showing or revealing *what* one is speaking about, *what* one is discussing . . . In such acts of revealing, whatever one is speaking about shows up, becomes perceivable, and, as something perceived, gets *defined* in and by the discussion about it.

LQT: 6

According to Heidegger, the particular operation whereby a process of framing and exhibiting proceeds simultaneously, belongs entirely to λογος [*logos*], a word that literally means 'word' and that comes to be defined as discourse, language, logic and even rationality. It is in and by λογος that beings come to be taken out of their hiddenness and revealed in their unconcealment (BT: 262). This is, it should be noted, not merely a Heideggerian innovation but another return to philosophy's origins, specifically a crucial turning point in the life of Socrates. In Plato's *Phaedo*, a dialogue that narrates, among other things, the last moments of Socrates' life, the aged philosopher provides an account of where it all began. In reflecting on the origins of his endeavours, Socrates tells how he began by trying to follow the example established by his predecessors and sought wisdom in 'the investigation of nature' (Plato 1990: 96a). He describes how this undertaking, despite its initial attraction and his best efforts, continually led him adrift, how he eventually gave it up and how he finally decided on an alternative route by investigating the truth of things in λόγος. 'So I thought,' Socrates explains, 'I must have recourse to λόγος and examine in them the truth of things' (Plato 1990: 99e). In connecting truth as unconcealment to λόγος, therefore, Heidegger is not introducing a new concept into the western intellectual tradition but is once again returning and referring it to its Greek origins.[3]

'What is,' Heidegger argues in 'The Origin of the Work of Art,' 'is never of our making or even merely a product of our minds, as it might all too easily seem' (OWA: 53). Rather it is the case that what exists remains, for the most part, concealed and in need of being explicitly revealed as such. 'Much of the world,' Heidegger writes, 'stands in need of "revelation," of being un-covered and made known. In other words, much of the world and much of human existence is by and large not un-covered. So beings can be un-covered or un-hidden. This uncoveredness or unhiddenness of beings is what we call truth' (LQT: 6). Or, as it is famously described in the text of *Being and Time*, 'Truth (uncoveredness) is something that must always first be wrested from entities. Entities get snatched out of their unhiddenness. The factical uncoveredness of anything is always, as it were, a kind of robbery' (BT: 265).

This alternative formulation of truth will necessarily change the way we understand and investigate language in particular and all mediated forms of representation in general. Contrary to the standard formulation – a formulation that already endorses the default position of the correspondence theory and that persists in standard approaches to semiotics, communication theory and Media Studies – it is not the case that there is a real world of existing things and then words, images and other forms of representation that are subsequently used to refer to and 'to say something about' these things. The structure and order of precedence between words and things must (as we have already seen in chapter 1) be significantly reconfigured. Understood in this fashion, 'representations', whether in the form of spoken discourse, descriptions provided by the ink and paper of print media, the analogue imaging technologies of photography and cinema or newly introduced forms of digital media and information technology, are not merely instruments that simply and passively convey information about a pre-existing real world but reveal through a kind of snatching and robbing, in and by λόγος, what is (the) real. For this reason, 'telling the truth' is not a matter of representing things adequately – typically measured by comparing a representation either to the Real thing (realism) or to other representations (idealism) – but of participating in the uncovering and disclosing of the being of things in the first place. Or as Heidegger succinctly summarizes, 'assertion communicates entities in the "how" of their uncoveredness' (BT: 266).

This does not mean, it should again be emphasized, that Heidegger simply endorses a naive brand of constitutionalism or linguistic idealism whereby things do not exist apart from or outside of the various means and mechanisms of representation. As Heidegger clearly states, 'things are, and human beings, gifts, and sacrifices are, animals and plants are, equipment and works are' (OWA: 52–3). Rather, it means that these 'things' are not simply given or immediately available in some kind of raw or naked state. What they are and how we understand what they are is something that is always and already unconcealed through a *logical* process by which they come to show themselves as such:

> To see this, only the right concept of language is needed. In the current view, language is held to be a kind of communication. It serves for verbal exchange and agreement, and in general for communicating. But language is not only and not primarily an audible and written expression of what is to be communicated. It not only puts forth in words and statements what is overtly or covertly intended to be communicated; language alone brings what is, as something that is, into the Open for the first time ... Language, by naming beings for the first time, first brings beings to word and to appearance. Only this naming nominates beings *to* their being *from out of* their being. (OWA: 73)

As we have seen previously (chapter 1), *language* for Heidegger is *not just a means* or instrument for communicating information about things; it also has a more original or constitutive dimension that discloses beings by bringing what is into the open in the first place. For this reason, language and other forms of media, or what is often called 'means of expression', should not be looked at as mere pale reflections of a pre-existing world of real things. Instead 'one must', as Carey argues, 'examine communication, even scientific communication, even mathematical expression, as the primary phenomena of experience and not as something "softer" and derivative from a "realer" existent nature' (1989: 26).

Consequently, what has been called Communication Studies or Media Studies needs to avoid seeing itself as a mode of evaluating the adequacy of a representation to the 'primary' reality that it is supposedly derived from and that it is said to represent. Instead, more systematic attention is required to the ways in which the means of available communication participate in the uncovering and revealing of what is. This fundamental change in perspective will, as Carey points out, necessarily mobilize an entirely different set of interests and research questions for scholars of media: 'How do we do this? What are the differences between these forms? What are the historical and comparative variations in them? How do changes in communication technology influence what we can concretely create and apprehend? How do groups in society struggle over the definition of what is real?' (1989: 26). This is the unique way of thinking that Heidegger introduces, develops and makes available to us.

CONCLUSION: CORRESPONDING WITH MCLUHAN

The two points that began this chapter (the theoretical distinction between the terms 'correct' and 'true' and the suggestion that what is true may become hidden due to an over-abundance of the correct) also apply to the reception of Heidegger's own work. There are various correct appreciations that emphasize how he pursues unconventional modes of thought and can, for that reason, be difficult to read. But this sort of appreciation frequently serves to deflect or displace the truth – the challenging new perspectives concerning the question of truth that are opened up when we apply his efforts and concerns to the media. Consequently, Heidegger's questioning of truth supplies four very useful and revealing insights that effectively challenge, if not completely rewrite, the rules of media's game of mediation:

1. Heidegger explains in considerable detail the theory of truth that is already assumed and deployed by media theory and practice. He not only characterizes the elements and operations of the 'correspondence theory of truth' but locates the development of this default setting within the history of western thought. This kind of detailed analysis would, by itself, be a major contribution to the field, but Heidegger always takes things further . . .

2. Heidegger submits this default understanding to a thorough critical investigation. He does this not because the usual way of doing things has been somehow wrong or inappropriate but because 'correspondence' cannot provide a complete account of its own theoretical perspective. There are, in other words, things that are presumed and operationalized by the correspondence theory that have remained – for most of its two thousand-year run – unquestioned and unexamined. In particular, Heidegger demonstrates how correspondence and the correctness of representation – in either its idealist or realist form – needs and requires a prior disclosure of being in order to have something against which to compare assertions and make evaluations about the truth or falsity of what is asserted.

3. To develop this critical insight further, Heidegger formulates a more original account of truth, one that is prior to correspondence in both conceptual structure and historical development. This formulation leverages the ancient Greek word ἀλήθεια [*aletheia*] and re-establishes truth on the ground of an original *unconcealing* from which correspondence eventually derives as a secondary aspect and side effect.

4. Heidegger assigns the work of unconcealing to λόγος [*logos*], another Greek word that is translated by a sequence of related terms: speech, language, logic, reason. In doing

so he completely reworks the assumed relationship situated between words and things such that telling the truth is no longer a matter of the correctness of representation but is involved with the very revealing of being. As a result, the media and material of representation are not instruments of communication or secondary phenomena that relate information about entities that are already 'out there' but are direct and active participants in revealing the being of those things that we subsequently think they merely represent.

Heidegger's importance for understanding media is illuminated by recounting two remarkable appearances of the media theorist Marshall McLuhan, who himself had situated Heidegger as a key figure for understanding contemporary media (McLuhan 1962: 280). The first occurs in a short but memorable scene from Woody Allen's 1977 Academy Award-winning film, *Annie Hall*. In the scene, the protagonist, Alvy Singer (Woody Allen), and his girlfriend, Annie Hall (Diane Keaton), are queuing to buy tickets to a film. Directly behind them is an academic who is pontificating *ad nauseam* to his companion about the films of Federico Fellini, the work of Samuel Beckett and the views of Marshall McLuhan. Alvy takes particular exception to this prattling. He steps out of the queue and registers his disapproval in a direct address to the camera: 'What do you do, when you get stuck in a movie line with a guy like this behind you?' The guy, who takes notice of the complaint, steps forward to confront his accuser: 'Wait a minute, why can't I give my opinion? It's a free country!' 'Do you have to give it so loud?' Alvy asks. 'I mean, aren't you ashamed to pontificate like that? And the funny part of it is, Marshall McLuhan – you don't know anything about Marshall McLuhan.' The man responds to this accusation by proudly proclaiming that he happens to teach a course at Columbia University called 'TV, Media, and Culture' and that his 'insights into Mr McLuhan have a great deal of validity.' 'Oh, do you?' Alvy replies. 'Well, that's funny because I happen to have Mr McLuhan right here.' And he steps to the edge of the frame to pull Marshall McLuhan out from behind a large, free-standing sign. McLuhan then admonishes the academic: 'I've heard what you're saying; you know nothing of my work ... How you got to teach a course in anything is totally amazing.' Satisfied with this result, Alvy once again addresses the camera: 'Boy, if life were only like this.'

This is precisely Heidegger's point. We do want life to be like this. We want to be able to measure and to evaluate what is asserted in comparison to the real thing as it actually is. The problem of course, and the point of Allen's joke, is that life is nothing like this. The correspondence theory of truth is more the exception than the rule. It is, in fact, not 'true' according to its own standard of correspondence and is instead more a product of what the US TV character Stephen Colbert calls 'truthiness' – something we have wanted to be true and attempt to make true by force of mutual agreement. Stating this, however, does not mean that the correspondence theory is simply *false*, which would amount to using the correspondence theory to disqualify and discount the theory itself. This is definitely not Heidegger's position. For Heidegger, it is not the case that the correspondence theory is somehow 'wrong', 'false' or 'inaccurate'. It is just not entirely sufficient in so far as it is supported by a more primordial and fundamental mode of disclosure.

The second notable appearance of McLuhan occurred almost twenty years after the release of *Annie Hall* and marks the conceptual limit of a certain brand of naive empiricism or expectation of objectivity that continues to exert a considerable influence on Communication Studies. In January 1996, *Wired* magazine published a rather surprising 'interview' with their self-proclaimed 'patron saint'. The interview was surprising because at the time it was conducted, McLuhan had been deceased for over a decade. According to the article's introduction: 'About a year ago, someone calling himself Marshall McLuhan began posting anonymously on a popular mailing list called Zone (zone@wired.com). Gary Wolf [the author of the article] began a correspondence with the poster via a chain of anonymous remailers' (Wolf 1996: 1).

In the spirit of this chapter, it is somewhat misguided to reduce consideration of this situation to notions of 'truthful correspondence', that is, whether the online interlocutor who Wolf described as having 'an eerie command of McLuhan's life and inimitable perspective' (1996: 1) was in fact McLuhan. A correctness-informed need to confirm that the literal act of correspondence (the exchange of emails) in turn corresponds with a real McLuhan at the other end misses a much richer philosophical truth: the resonance such an exchange has with a more figurative understanding of media technology as a ready realm for ghosts as portrayed by Geoffrey Bennington and Jacques Derrida (1993 [1991]: 347), Friedrich Kittler (1999 [1986]) and Avital Ronell (1989). In this instance, there was no way to reach outside the edge of the frame and draw the real thing (McLuhan caught in the act of typing) into the field of vision so that it would show itself as itself, as was the case with Alvy Singer's exhibition of McLuhan in *Annie Hall*.

For this reason, most respectable journalists and media organizations would have pulled the story. However, instead of dismissing the whole affair as ultimately unverifiable, *Wired* published the interview under the rather clever title 'Channeling McLuhan'. In doing so, they took what was arguably a Heideggerian approach to things, focusing attention not on the potential 'fallacies' of the situation but on what could be revealed in the process of the discursive exchange. The editors of *Wired* explained, 'after many rounds of email, the conversation got down to the meat of the matter: What does McLuhan think about all this new digital technology?' (Wolf 1996: 1). This does not mean, it should be emphasized once again, that questions of validity and correctness of representation in matters regarding media are somehow wrong or impertinent. This is not the point – not for Heidegger, nor presumably for *Wired* magazine. Questions of validity, correspondence and agreement remain operational and have a considerable amount of historical weight behind them. Heidegger's point is simply that there is more to it than this. There is another, more 'profound' way to engage the question of truth. And if we remain at the more 'superficial' level of correspondence, we not only miss something essential but conceal what can be revealed by thinking truth as unconcealment and what this tells us about the mediation of *things*.

3

IN MEDIAS RES

INTRODUCTION: FIRST THINGS FIRST

Meanings inspired only by remote, confused, inauthentic
intuitions – if by any intuitions at all – are not enough: we
must go back to 'the things themselves'.

Husserl 1975 [1970]: 252

Heidegger's doctrine of the thing is a puzzling combination
of deep insights and idiosyncratic esotericism.

Feenberg 1999: 194

What is a thing? We all know what things are; we deal with
them every day. Indeed, one way to characterize being in time
is by the colloquialism 'Same thing, different day.' Things
are and persist across time. Some things stay the same; other
things change from one day to the next. Despite this, no one,
or almost no one it seems, would be confused, confounded or
perplexed as to what a thing is. Yet, as Husserl (Heidegger's

teacher) points out above, authentic understanding requires that *we must go back to the things themselves*. In Heidegger's terms, we need to pay close attention to our dealings with entities *within-the-world*. If we do not, there is a very real risk that, by taking things for granted (in a very literal sense), we allow ourselves to be governed by 'remote, confused, inauthentic intuitions'. The danger of succumbing to such intuitions is particularly important when one considers that, as we have previously emphasized, the media mediate; they position themselves between us and things in ways we frequently do not perceive or acknowledge.

'The question of things, Heidegger remarks at the beginning of a 1935/6 lecture course later published as *Die Frage nach dem Ding* [*The Question Concerning the Thing*], is one of the most ancient, venerable, and fundamental problems of metaphysics' (Benso 2000: 59). Notwithstanding the importance Heidegger imputes to the question 'What is a thing?', he is well aware that it appears, at least on the face of things, to be an absurd if not comical inquiry. In fact, at the beginning of the lecture, the normally sober and serious Heidegger engages with the comic aspects of this question by doing something quite uncharacteristic – he tells a joke or what he calls 'a little story . . . Plato has preserved in the *Theaetetus*':

> The story is that Thales, while occupied in studying the heavens above and looking up, fell into a well. A good-looking and whimsical maid from Thrace laughed at him and told him that while he might passionately want to know all things in the universe, the things in front of his very nose and feet were unseen by him. Plato added to this story the remark: 'This jest also fits all those who become involved in philosophy.' Therefore, the question, 'What is a thing?' must always be rated as one which causes housemaids to

laugh. And genuine housemaids must have something to laugh about. (WIT: 3)

This is, as is often said of observational humour, 'funny because it is true'.

The question 'What is a thing?' appears to be one of those inquiries that causes philosophy to look bad, or at least comical. Only philosophy could get hung up on this question as it is only philosophers who gaze into the heavens pondering 'all things in the universe' and, in the process, inevitably miss what is closest at hand and already directly under their noses. Everyone else, even the housekeeper, knows what things are and has no problem identifying and dealing with them. It is only the philosopher who gets tripped up and finds himself falling into wells or worse. Despite this danger (or perhaps precisely because of it), Heidegger is willing to risk tripping up and looking stupid. He does so because the question 'What is a thing?' is something that is just too important, influential and pivotal to be passed over in silence. As if learning from and answering to the laughter of the housemaid in Plato's story, Heidegger eschews gazing into the heavens at distant things and prefers to pay attention to what is close by and already 'right under our noses'. In this spirit, this chapter's exploration of Heidegger's analysis of things helps to address one of this book's primary themes – a philosophically informed understanding of the media environment that lies right under contemporary readers' noses but which normally escapes full recognition. Of all things, media repay close philosophical attention because, in the context of Heidegger's radical questioning of our most basic assumptions about things, they serve a uniquely complex and influential role, functioning as they do between the realms of inanimate objects (the technological apparatus of the HD television screen, the smartly designed smartphone, the digital camera and MP3 player, etc.) and representation (the high-definition computer-generated images, the surround-sound audio or the augmented reality they are built to convey).

Despite being only intermittently mentioned by Heidegger himself, media encapsulate practical and updated illustrations of many of his key concepts. More than this, in an increasingly digitalized society in which life is pervasively mediated to an unprecedented level to fulfil Marx's claim that 'all that is solid melts into air', Heidegger's phenomenological analysis of things has never been more relevant. Particularly pertinent for a networked digital society, he moves beyond the seemingly self-evident, but ultimately incomplete, understanding of things as entities or objects. Instead, he provides a much richer phenomenological account of how *thingness* is in fact inextricably related to human concerns and dealings that occur in a distinctly insubstantial and non-thing-like fashion. In doing so, Heidegger illuminates the seemingly intangible, but actually fundamental, phenomenological aspects of *mediated* things – those things we commonly experience as 'equipment'.

THE THING ABOUT EQUIPMENT

The Greeks had an appropriate term for 'Things': πράγματα [pragmata] – that is to say, that which one has to do with in one's concernful dealings (πρᾶξις). But ontologically, the specific 'pragmatic' character of the πράγματα is just what the Greeks left in obscurity; they thought of these 'proximally' as 'mere Things'. We shall call those entities which we encounter in concern '*equipment*' [*Zeug*].

BT: 96–7

The cursory over-familiarity with which we tend to use common expressions like 'taking things for granted' and the 'simplest of things' illustrates the immediate problems encountered when we try to analyse the misleadingly obvious character of things. The words we use simultaneously recognize things but miss their 'thingness'. Heidegger's initial engagement with 'the thing' occurs in *Being and Time* where, as can be seen above, he goes back to the roots of the western philosophical tradition to point out the blind spot that exists when it comes to considering the true phenomenological nature of our relationship to things. Heidegger points out that, for the Ancient Greeks, useful everyday objects, *pragmata*, were viewed as 'mere things' but that this dismissive 'mere' obscures an underlying significance – an obscuring of things that continues to exist today, especially if one thinks of how 'being pragmatic' connotes 'merely' doing what a situation requires. Hence, both then and now, the pragmatic resides in a realm subordinated to apparently loftier concerns. Here as elsewhere, however, Heidegger turns things on their head. Rather than sidelining the pragmatic, he takes loftier concerns right back to their pragmatic roots, or to put it in another, deliberately reflexive and disorientating way, we need to be more pragmatic about what we usually consider to be merely pragmatic.

The Ancient Greeks' approach emphasizes how far back in western culture the tendency to overlook things goes. By contrast, Heidegger emphasizes concepts like 'concern' and 'equipment' to refocus our attention upon those phenomenological qualities of things that go beyond their overlooked status as insignificant nearby objects. He seeks to investigate how the things we use are already innately related to larger totalities which, although not physically present in the-thing-itself, nevertheless play a key role in structuring our dealings with that entity. This rather unique approach to things characterizes Heidegger's particular method of operationalizing Husserl's dictum to go back *to the things themselves*. Rather than merely looking *at* things or trying to gaze into their hidden recesses, Heidegger advocates the investigation of everyday involvements, our *dealings*, with which we find ourselves already engaged *with* entities within-the-world. In this way, everything is what it is in having a *for which* or a destination *to which* it is always and already referred. Things are – they first come to be what they are – in being useful for some task and by being put to use for some specific purpose.

But Heidegger, as he almost always does, takes things one step further. It is not the case, he points out, that we encounter these pieces of equipment individually and in a mode of differentiated singularity. If we are attentive to the actual situation (if, in other words, we are good phenomenologists or empirical researchers), we discover that our involvements and encounters with equipment always and already occur within a totality of interrelated things. To illustrate this, Heidegger uses the example of his study, a room that is ostensibly filled with various pieces of equipment, such as pens, paper, a table and chair, a lamp, and so on. These 'things', Heidegger argues, are never encountered and appear to us in isolation such that they accumulate and come to fill up the room. Instead, what we encounter – what is immediately available to us – is the totality of the room. Not as some contained space situated between four walls, but as a totality of equipment useful for living and working (BT: 97–8). Consequently, what is encountered first and foremost is an undifferentiated totality of things, and it is from this prior 'arrangement', and out of our involvements and dealings in this totality, that an individual piece of equipment eventually emerges and shows itself as such. In the terminology developed in the previous chapter, it could be said that this explains how the being of some thing comes to be plucked out of its undifferentiated entanglement in its environment and exhibited as being a particular thing. Exactly how this transpires and what it means is something that is further developed and explicated by way of Heidegger's analysis of *Zuhandenheit* or the *ready-to-hand*.

READY-TO-HAND, OR HOW EVERYTHING IS MEDIA

The ontological status or the kind of being that belongs to such *equipment* is primarily exhibited as 'ready-to-hand' or *Zuhandenheit*, meaning that some-thing becomes what it is or acquires its properly 'thingly character' when we use it for some particular purpose.

BT: 98

According to Heidegger, the ontological status or the kind of being that belongs to equipment is primarily exhibited as 'ready-to-hand', meaning that something becomes what it is or acquires its properly 'thingly character' in coming to be put to work for some particular purpose. A hammer, one of Heidegger's principal examples, is for hammering; a pen is for writing; a shoe is for wearing. Everything is what it is in having a *for which* or a destination to which it is always and already referred. Perhaps a useful way to understand the importance of the ready-to-hand is to think of it as expressing *that which lies in things more than the things themselves*. In other words, things are not primarily encountered by just staring at their outward appearance in order to see them for what they are. They are – they first come to be what they are – in being useful for some task and by being assigned to or put to use for some specific purpose. Even in the case of apparently 'useless' artworks, use is derived from art's very uselessness (Kant's notion of purposiveness without purpose).

This characterization of things is a crucial one for

understanding our relationship to media, and Heidegggger's account can be related to the work of a number of thinkers more easily recognized as media theorists. It is, for example, similar to that portrayed by Walter Benjamin in his influential 1936 essay *The Work of Art in the Age of Mechanical Reproduction*. Seeking to describe the unprecedented scale and range of the new forms of sense perception facilitated by the advent of mass media, Benjamin relies on a comparison with architecture. He suggests (positively) that we experience technologies like cinema in a state of *distraction* akin to our interaction with buildings in which we naturally and unaffectedly reside. Using a similar notion, but with a much more pessimistic tone, Kracauer observes that:

> Out of the hubbub, rise the newspaper kiosks, tiny temples in which the publications of the entire world get together for a rendezvous ... But, alas, these newspapers do not know one another. Each copy is folded in on itself and is content to read its own columns. Regardless of the close physical relations that the papers cultivate, their news is so completely lacking in any contact that they are uninformed about one another. In the interstices the demon of absent-mindedness reigns supreme. (Kracauer 1995 [1963]: 43)

Using phrases like 'the "content" of a medium is like the juicy piece of meat carried by the burglar to distract the watchdog of the mind', McLuhan (1995: 32) also identified the way media tend to be unreflexively self-consumed and he deployed and developed the implications that Heidegger's concept of the ready-to-hand has for our understanding of the media (*Understanding Media* being the title of McLuhan's most substantial piece of work). In McLuhan's hands, 'media' becomes a term that is not restricted to the usual suspects: newspapers, radio, television, and so on. Instead, the concept is defined more generally (Heidegger would say 'ontologically') as 'an extension' of human capabilities and involvements (McLuhan 1995: 4). Now iconic, his examples include: the wheel as an extension of the foot, the telephone as an extension of the ear, and television as an extension of the eye. Although not mentioning McLuhan by name, Paul Dourish effectively connects the dots between these two thinkers by way of the computer mouse: 'As an example, consider the mouse connected to my computer. Much of the time, I act *through* the mouse; the mouse is an extension of my hand as I select objects, operate menus, and so forth. The mouse is, in Heidegger's terms, ready-to-hand' (Dourish 2004: 109).

In *Being and Time*, the mode of being that belongs to things appears as 'a using *of* something for something' (BT: 100). 'This does not necessarily mean,' as Silvia Benso explains, 'that all things are tools, instruments which *Dasein* effectively uses and exploits, but rather that they disclose themselves to *Dasein* as endowed with some form of significance for its own existence and tasks' (Benso 2000: 79). A profound consequence of readiness-to-hand, therefore, is that everything is what it is and has its own unique being only in so far as it is always and already accommodated to and comprehended by *Dasein*, and the term thus encapsulates those things that we encounter as pre-prepared to be part of our concernful dealings. Readiness-to-hand is therefore not just a temporary attitude or viewpoint we adopt with regards to things. It acts to define the very being of things as things. 'Readiness-to-hand,' Heidegger argues, 'is the way in which entities as they are "in themselves" are defined ontologico-categorially' (BT: 101).

So what does this mean for our investigation of media? Everything. This is because something ready-to-hand is situated and conceptualized as a kind of intermediary or medium. Things are and come to be what they are first and foremost as equipment, instruments and a means to an end (and the full implications of understanding things as a 'means to an end' will be explored in the next chapter). For this reason, media will not be just one thing or one kind of thing. All things, in so far as they are something rather than nothing, are always and already *media*. A key consequence of this insight is that what might appear to be our otherwise seemingly neutral interactions with things are in fact preconditioned a priori with/by a highly naturalized perception of purpose or an 'in-order-to'. This is a process of *mediation* that characterizes *Dasein*'s mode of being-in-the-world with those entities that, as we shall continue to discuss throughout the rest of this book, are of particular relevance to media, those things the innate purpose of which is, unsurprisingly, to *mediate*.

If all of this seems a bit difficult to grasp, it is because whatever is ready-to-hand is essentially transparent, unremarkable and even invisible. The paradox of the ready-to-hand is therefore the fact that in its most authentic form, it necessarily withdraws from direct view. In our everyday dealings and concerns, we focus on the work that has to be done rather than the particular tools that we use to carry out that work (BT: 99). Or as Michael Zimmerman explains by way of Heidegger's hammer, 'In hammering away at the sole of a shoe, the cobbler *does not notice the hammer*. Instead, the tool is in effect transparent as an extension of his hand . . . For tools to work right, they must be "invisible," in the sense that they disappear in favor of the work being done' (1990: 139). The same can be said of media. Media work – or they effectively mediate – in so far as they are not seen as such but recede from view providing viewers/readers/listeners access to whatever content they are designed to deliver. We do not, in other words, watch the television set; we watch the football match, the news documentary, or the dramatic programme it conveys. Consequently, what is 'authentically' handy is something that withdraws or recedes from view, allowing one to *see through it* in order to accomplish some particular task. 'For concernful Dasein,' Rudolf Bernet explains, 'the proper use of things consists in letting itself be carried along by these references without stopping to think about them. . . . Efficacious understanding of a thing's sense consists precisely in its being a matter of course and passing unnoticed' (1994: 260). This, however, raises the question of what is happening when we do notice things.

PRESENT-AT-HAND AND TECHNICAL DIFFICULTIES . . . PLEASE STAND BY

The modes of conspicuousness, obtrusiveness, and obstinacy all have the function of bringing to the fore the characteristic of presence-at-hand in what is ready-to-hand.

BT: 104

Obstinacy, *conspicuousness* and *obtrusiveness* are terms Heidegger uses to describe the conditions whereby we are jolted out of our experience of the ready-to-hand. It is often in moments of failure that we perceive our equipment to be conspicuous, when, for example, the power goes out during the big game and we stare dumbfoundedly at the blank screen of the television. Or, in terms of obstinacy, think of the character Basil Fawlty from the UK television programme *Fawlty Towers* who in one memorable scene started beating his Mini Cooper with a tree branch out of sheer frustration at its 'wilful' refusal to start.[1] In other words, things conspicuously and obtrusively stand out as objects of direct contemplation when they cease to be useful or 'handy' (again, our common expressions are more philosophically significant than we often recognize). In these circumstances, things come to be disclosed as merely 'present-at-hand' or *Vorhandenheit*. This mode of being is, strictly speaking, derived, deficient and negative. What is merely present-at-hand becomes available and shows itself as such only when something has become *un-ready-to-hand* (BT: 103).

Our technical devices – cars, washing machines, televisions, smartphones, etc. – usually only appear to us as such when there are technical difficulties or breakdowns in the normal and assumed smooth functioning of the apparatus (Figure 3.1). In these exceptional moments, the device stands out before us as an obvious, obtrusive, and even, as in Basil Fawlty's case, an obnoxious object. In fact the word 'object' is particularly resonant in this context. An object, or in Heidegger's German *Gegenstand*, is quite literally something that is thrown (ject) or stands (*stand*) in opposition (ob/gegen) to us. In the event of technical difficulties, for example, the television *stands out* and opposes our concernful absorption. As long as it works, a television acts as a 'window on the world' for what we can see in it, but as a thing itself it recedes from our view. In fact, it was to cater to the obtrusive nature of the turned-off TV television set that early televisions were housed in large wooden cabinets that seamlessly fitted in with the rest of the living room furniture. Today, by contrast, it is the ultra-thin profile of the plasma screen that enables the apparatus to recede into the wall upon which it hangs.

Something becomes present-at-hand when the thing in question fails to work, breaks down or interrupts the smooth functioning of what had been already handy and ready-to-hand. 'The equipmental character of things is explicitly apprehended,' Benso writes, '*via negativa* when a thing reveals its unusability, or is missing, or "stands in the way" of *Dasein*'s concern' (Benso 2000: 82). For Heidegger, there are three modes or ways by which this occurs:

Figure 3.1 Two recognizable images of technical breakdown: the 'Please Stand By' of broadcast television and the Windows OS 'Blue Screen of Death'

1. *Conspicuousness*: Something is conspicuous when it becomes unusable, that is, when it no longer unproblematically serves the use for which it was designed (BT: 102). The experience of conspicuousness occurs when something that had been useful and ready-to-hand for some task becomes obviously unusable or unready-to-hand (BT: 102–3). In the case of Dourish's computer mouse, when everything functions as it should, the mouse is an inconspicuous 'extension of my hand as I select objects, operate menus, and so forth'.

> Sometimes, however, such as when I reach the edge of the mouse pad and cannot move the mouse further, my orientation toward the mouse changes. Now I become conscious of the mouse mediating my action, precisely because of the fact that it has been interrupted. The mouse becomes the object of my attention as I pick it up and move it back to the center of the mouse pad. When I act on the mouse in this way, being mindful of it as an object of my activity, the mouse is *present-at-hand*. (Dourish 2004: 109)

2. *Obtrusiveness*: Something is or becomes obtrusive, when it is missing. 'In our concernful dealings,' Heidegger explains, 'we not only come up against unusable things within what is ready-to-hand already: we also find things which are missing – which not only are not "handy" but are not "to hand" at all' (BT: 103). Car keys often obtrude in this fashion. Usually we go through our daily routine unaware of the keys. They withdraw from direct view in so far as they already are usable things that are ready-to-hand for the purposes of transportation. We leave the apartment, jump into our car and fight traffic to get to our destination. But as soon as they are missing, lost in the cushions of the couch, for instance, then we take explicit notice of them as missing. In these situations, what had been virtually invis-

ible as ready-to-hand now obtrudes *in abstentia* as something present-at-hand.

3. *Obstinacy*: There are also things that get in the way, things that do not yield to our involvements and that interrupt our activities. Such things stubbornly '"stand in the way" of our concern' (BT: 103). Consider, for example, the *jump cut* in film and video editing. The classic Hollywood approach to editing developed in such a way that the cut from one shot to another is seamless and transparent, thus creating the appearance of uninterrupted temporal and spatial continuity. In 'continuity editing', as it is called, the cut is typically situated in order that there is a 'match on action' from the viewpoint of one camera position to the next, so that there is (or at least appears to be) an uninterrupted flow of action in time. In addition, this approach to editing generally respects what is called the '180-degree rule', which restricts the camera from crossing an imaginary line drawn between the subjects of the scene in an effort to maintain spatial continuity between different camera positions. This is, in particular, one of the techniques that help to ensure that two characters in dialogue 'face' each other and appear to occupy the same space. The jump cut, evidenced in Sergei Eisenstein's *Battleship Potemkin* (1925), Jean-Luc Godard's renowned debut *Breathless* (1960) and virtually every music video ever made, deliberately interrupts and disturbs this approach to editing. As the name suggests, the jump cut introduces temporal discontinuities by intentionally disturbing match-on-action or on-screen spatial continuity by jumping over the 180-degree line. By doing so, the cut 'stands in the way' of the on-screen action and, in this obstinacy, stands out as something present-at-hand, or, it may be more accurate to say, we experience it as present-at-hand unless the editing technique itself becomes a naturalized part of our viewing experience and no longer gets in the way of the

narrative flow. Think, for example, of both the jerky camera action and jump cuts pioneered by such television shows as *NYPD Blue*; initially highly disorientating, these techniques are arguably now part of our ready-to-hand viewing experience.

Heidegger's distinction between presence-to-hand and readiness-to-hand has profound, if not revolutionary, implications for the way in which we understand the media. For the philosophers who come before him – and we are talking about a long line of influential thinkers that go back to Plato – things have often been investigated abstractly, as merely present-at-hand. In fact, philosophers typically think about things by stripping away all their accidental properties, investments of value and especially the practical employments to which they have been applied. A seminal example of this method is found in the work of René Descartes, who famously argued that everything we commonly associate with a particular thing, like a piece of wax – namely its visual appearance, its tactile qualities, its colour, its odour, etc. – is in fact immaterial to what that thing really is (Descartes 1988 [1983]: 84–5). In fact, after having effectively doubted every aspect that is or can be obtained by way of the senses, Descartes concludes that a thing, like the wax, 'consists not in its being something which is hard or heavy or coloured, or which affects the senses in any way, but simply in its being something which is extended in length, breadth and depth' (Descartes 1988 [1983]: 190).

Descartes, as Heidegger is acutely aware, was practising the kind of cognitive abstraction that was targeted and ridiculed in the story from Plato's *Theaetetus*. For this reason, 'Descartes' conception of the world,' Heidegger concludes, 'is ontologically defective ... his interpretation and the foundations on which it is based have led him to pass over both the phenomenon of the world and the Being of those entities within-the-world which are proximally ready-to-hand' (BT: 128). Instead of proceeding along the path of theoretical abstraction taken by figures like Descartes and Kant, Heidegger charts a course in the opposite direction, beginning with everyday practical involvements, the mode of *concernful absorption*, whereby things are not encountered as obtrusive, conspicuous or obstinate entities, but rather seamlessly as ready-to-hand. The more abstract mode of disclosure, what Heidegger calls 'presence-at-hand', is thereby situated as a subsequent and derived mode of the being of things.

THE QUESTION CONCERNING MEDIATED THINGS

When we let the thing in its thinging essence from out of the worlding world, then we commemorate the thing as thing. Thinking in this way we are met by the thing as thing. We are, in the strict sense of the word, conditioned. We have left the arrogance of everything unconditional behind us.

BFL: 19

Although in his early writing Heidegger claims that 'the thingness must be something unconditioned' (WIT: 9), as can be seen above, he subsequently realized the need to leave 'the arrogance of everything unconditional behind us'. Because of his ongoing struggle to conceive of things in their thingness whilst simultaneously recognizing the world disclosing aspects of *Dasein*, the question of the thing continued to be an important matter for Heidegger, if not something of an obsession. It reappears in the 1930s with 'What is a thing?' and 'The Origin of the Work of Art' but the apex of Heidegger's thinking on this topic is situated in the post-war period with a short essay called 'The Thing'. Published in 1954, 'The Thing' originally took shape as the first of the 1949 Bremen Lectures, *Insight into That Which Is*, Heidegger's first official speaking engagement after the end of the Second World War. If Heidegger had, since resigning the rector-ship of Freiburg University in the mid-1930s, mainly kept to himself, producing what might be called 'secret writings' (Ruin 2005: 358), the Bremen Lectures show him cautiously returning to public life. But most importantly, this series of four lectures contained initial versions of three pivotal essays that have come to define the later Heidegger: 'The Thing', 'The Question Concerning Technology' and 'The Turning'.

The published version of 'The Thing' and the general introduction to the Bremen Lectures, entitled 'The Point of Reference', commence with Heidegger doing something rather uncharacteristic – addressing communications media in general and the technology of television in particular. In Heidegger's eyes, as was highlighted in our Introduction, the general significance and effects of telecommunications is immediately evident – they foreclose and even annihilate physical distance and delay. In the face of this historically unprecedented situation, Heidegger asks a series of probing and insightful questions:

> What is happening here when, as a result of the abolition of great distances, everything is equally far and equally near? What is this uniformity in which everything is neither far nor near – is, as it were, without distance? Everything gets lumped together into uniform distancelessness. How? Is not this merging of everything into the distanceless more unearthly than everything bursting apart? (TT: 166)

For Heidegger, this unearthly distancelessness concerns things. Despite the fact that, due to the media of telecommunications, all distance seems to be shrinking and everything is apparently coming closer together, it is precisely *the thing* – the thing as a thing – that remains farthest away and out of reach. 'Nearness,' Heidegger writes, 'apparently cannot be encountered directly. We succeed in reaching it rather by attending to what is near. Near to us are what we usually call things. But what is a thing? Man has so far given no more thought to the thing as a thing than he has to nearness' (TT: 166). For this reason, Heidegger finds it once again prudent to ask the basic, even remedial question 'What is a thing?'

The first step in responding to this question is to differentiate the thing from an *object*. This effort calls upon and mobilizes a long-standing philosophical distinction between objects and things. Within German philosophy, the point of contact for this is Immanuel Kant. In his landmark work *Critique of Pure Reason* (first published in 1781 and revised in 1787), Kant famously distinguished the object, which appears to us through the mediation of our senses, from the thing-in-itself, which remains always and forever inaccessible and remote. An object, as Heidegger explains (and as we have seen above), takes up its place opposite us, and in opposition to us, either by being immediately presented through perception or by being recollected as a mental image or re-presentation (literally 'presented again'). For this reason, things are not, in and of themselves, objects; they become objects by being situated opposite a subject or in opposition to a subject. As Heidegger aphoristically expresses it in the third of the Bremen Lectures, 'what stands over against is the object for the subject' (BFL: 37).

Although Heidegger does not explicitly say so in 'The Thing', this consideration of the object is clearly related to what had been developed in *Being and Time*. As something that is initially ready-to-hand, things always and already withdraw into *Dasein*'s concernful dealings with the world.

Such equipment is immediately handy; the thing does not stand in the way or oppose us in any way whatsoever. It is, therefore, not (yet) an object. However, that which comes to be present-at-hand, either in the mode of conspicuousness, obtrusiveness or obstinacy, does in fact become an explicit object of representation the minute it stands out or gets in the way of our concern. As we have previously pointed out, our various media devices – laptop computers, smart phones, tablets or televisions – do not become an object of explicit contemplation as long as we are able to access online applications, watch videos or download music. These things only obtrude and become a conspicuous object when they fail to work and stand out over and against us. The *screen*, therefore, acts unobtrusively as both a noun and a verb. Functioning as a noun, it is the unremarked surface upon which is displayed various kinds of digital data and, as a verb, it shields us from contemplating the whole technical apparatus in its own right.

Consequently, from the perspective of 'The Thing', *Being and Time* is not so much about 'things in their thingness' as it is about objects and the process of objectification. Pornography (the perennial cutting-edge application for all new media technologies from daguerreotypes to the internet) provides an insightful object lesson. The 'problem with pornography', as it is often described, is that it turns women (but not just women) into objects of sex. Pornography dehumanizes the other by representing her as a mere object for the enjoyment of some predominantly male subject. For this reason, leading critics of pornography, like Andrea Dworkin and Catherine A. MacKinnon, 'hold that the primary means of gender oppression is the objectification of women, and pornography exemplifies this objectification' (Scott 2005: 36). Although Heidegger says little about media in general and nothing about porn in particular, he is concerned with what he perceives to be the dominant force and controlling influence of this drive to objectification – science. In fact, science is, in terms of our everyday understanding of things, positively characterized as the model of and for 'objective knowledge'.

Defining what a thing is, a jug for instance (and this is Heidegger's principal and privileged example throughout the text of 'The Thing'), appears to be something that could certainly be provided by the science of physics. Although the 'vessel's thingness' appears to consist in what Heidegger calls the 'void that holds', 'physical science assures us that the jug is filled with air' and that when the vessel is filled with water or wine, the one liquid merely displaces the other (TT: 169–70). But science, Heidegger argues, does not approach the thing as thing. It only offers access to 'the objects of science'. 'The statements of physics are correct,' Heidegger admits. 'By means of them, science represents something real, by which it is objectively controlled. But – is this reality the jug? No. Science always encounters only what its kind of representation has admitted beforehand as an object possible for science' (TT: 170). In stating this, Heidegger is not, it is important to note, some knee-jerk anti-science critic by any means. What he wants to point out is that science works and does its work by turning everything into an object of experimental representation. By doing so, science is only able to grasp a highly constrained and isolated object and does not necessarily reach the thing itself.

A good example of this limitation is available with the recent discovery of the Higgs boson particle, or what has, perhaps unfortunately, been nominated the 'God particle'. Higgs boson is a proposed elementary particle in the standard model of particle physics, and it is theorized as the means by which the other elementary particles acquire mass. In the summer of 2012, scientists working with the Large Hadron Collider at CERN in Geneva, Switzerland ran a series of

experiments that produced data consistent with what would
be expected of the Higgs boson particle.

When well-meaning journalists asked the experimental team whether their findings were in fact the particle,
the physicists were careful to respond that what had been
discovered was data, ostensibly a form of representation,
which gave indication of the presence of an object that was
statistically consistent with the properties of the theorized
particle. Recognizing this kind of limitation, Heidegger
argues that 'science's knowledge, which is compelling
within its own sphere, the sphere of objects, already had
annihilated things as things.' In other words, within the
realm of objective, scientific knowledge, 'the thingness of
the thing remains concealed' (TT: 170). To return to 'The
Point of Departure', we can say that the forces of objectification contained within media and the physical sciences,
appear to bring distant and previously inaccessible things
increasingly closer, but in fact they only provide access to
objects.

HEIDEGGER'S OBJECTION TO OBJECTS

> The thinghood of the thing . . . does not reside in the thing
> becoming the object of a representation, nor can the thing-
> hood of the thing at all be determined by the objectivity
> of the object, not even when we take the opposition of the
> object as not simply due to our representation, but rather
> leave opposition to the object itself as its own affair.
>
> BFL: 5

Heidegger distinguishes between the thing as a thing and its
objectification in the form of an object (*Gegenstand*). Unlike
objects things 'do not appear *by means of* human making'
(TT: 181). They are independent or self-standing (*selbststän-*

dig). Using the example of a simple earthenware vessel to convey his complex thought, Heidegger writes that:

> the jug is a thing neither in the sense of the Roman *res*, nor in the sense of the medieval *ens*, let alone in the modern sense of object. The jug is a thing insofar as it things. The presence of something present such as the jug comes into its own, appropriatively manifests and determines itself, only from the thinging of the thing. (TT: 177)

The thing, Heidegger argues is nothing like what the Romans identified with the Latin word *res*, which is often translated as 'thing' but originally meant 'an affair, a contested matter, a case at law' (TT: 175). It also is not what the medieval European philosophers thought of in terms of *ens*, again a word that is often translated as 'thing' but initially referred to 'that which is present in the sense of standing forth here' (TT: 175). Nor is it properly identified as the *object* or *Gegenstand* of modern science. It is entirely otherwise. But what can Heidegger possibly mean by such curious and seemingly tautological phrases as 'the thingness of the thing' and 'the thinging of the thing?'

What Heidegger is doing here and elsewhere is no less radical than to think the thing in excess of all means of objective thought. In other words, he wants to conceptualize the thing outside the boundaries of all previously available modes of conceptualization. He wants to attend to the thing in such a way that exceeds the standard subject/object relationship whereby objects take up a position standing opposite an inquiring subject. Perhaps most alarmingly, he wants to say or represent something about things outside the realm of any and all possible forms of expression or representation. It is a seemingly impossible task, and it is one that will necessarily risk non-sense in so far as objective representation already works to constitute and define the very condition of possibility for making sense.

Armed as we are with such a vague catch-all and expressively inadequate term as 'thing',[2] it is difficult to see how else Heidegger could conduct his analysis without in some manner problematizing the unquestioned and seemingly natural way with which we normally conceptualize and describe things. He is after all attempting to analyse things in a way that the innate ready-to-hand nature of language militates against. Faced with the systemically objectifying properties of thought itself, Heidegger seeks to convey a mode of thinking that is prepared to grapple with the true implacable facticity of *things*, as opposed to objects. In principle a noble endeavour, a sense of its innate difficulty and iconoclastic nature can be gauged from the necessarily opaque mode of expression found throughout Heidegger's texts – a mode of expression that often and quite deliberately looks more like *poetry* than hard-headed, objective philosophical analysis (see chapter 1). This, however, is the price to be paid for achieving an authentic response to, and contrast with, the objectifying tendencies of which contemporary media are but the most recent (il)logical conclusion. It strives to provide a truly innovative account that is able to 'think outside the box' of objectification and to situate thought in the middle of things.

CONCLUSION: CRITICAL ASPECTS OF THIS THING CALLED MEDIA

One thing about which fish know exactly nothing is water, since they have no anti-environment which would enable them to perceive the element they live in.

McLuhan 1997: 175

Heidegger's multifaceted analysis of things has several important consequences for our investigation of this thing called media:

1. *The problem of transparency*: Immersed in our media-saturated world, like Marshall McLuhan's fish that knows nothing about water, we are often unable to see media as the 'things' they truly are. A Heidegger-informed appreciation of the media is therefore important for the way it calls attention to those aspects of mediation that are usually not seen as such, precisely because they function so seamlessly. Despite its co-optation as a catchy slogan by the same media system it aimed to critique, this remains the import of McLuhan's famous aphorism 'the medium is the message' (1995: 5). A Heideggerian-influenced understanding of the media enables us to intervene strategically in what is always and already ready-to-hand to make conspicuously present-at-hand what has hitherto been invisible. Consequently, Heidegger's distinction between *present-at-hand* and *ready-to-hand* contains a foundational insight for those seeking to engage in critical media studies. Because we often consume media as if they were transparent and invisible, the investigation of media can only proceed by first making them conspicuous, obtrusive or obstinate. There is, in this sense, a kind of necessary and unavoidable violation or violence involved in critical readings of the media – a kind of breaking or short-circuiting of the equipment in order to make it stand out as such so that a proper ontological understanding of its equipmentality can then be sought.

This approach questions the extent to which we can be circumspect (in the conventional sense) about Heidegger's precise notion of circumspection. Heidegger's concept requires that we don't just stare *at* the ready-to-hand as an abstract object but instead act concernfully *within* its orbit in order to operationalize a series of complex questions

concerning *Dasein*'s own concernful absorption in a heav-
ily mediated environment. Despite the fact that Heidegger
is clear that his account of ready-to-hand equipmentality in
Being and Time is ontological, there are equally clear indi-
cations of profound cultural implications that are highly
relevant to a society pervaded by multifarious technologies
of mediation.

2. *In medias res*: Whilst the analysis of *Being and Time*
had characterized all things as media, that is, the means by
which *Dasein* achieves the objective of his/her concernful
dealings with the world, the post-war writings ('The Thing'
in particular) demonstrate how things have already been
comprehended as objects of mediated representation. This
means that the situation initially described at the beginning
of the Bremen Lectures as 'The Point of Departure' is not
exceptional; it is the rule. What Heidegger identifies as
happening with communications media, namely an objectification of things that forecloses distance yet inevitably misses
the thing, leaving it untouched and inaccessible, is not something limited to what we typically recognize as the media
of communication but characterizes all forms of objective
representation up to and including scientific knowledge.
Consequently, the apparent effects of media are only a
symptom of a primordial and widespread mediation that has
already, from the very beginning, turned things into objects
of representation. It is, in other words, not the case that the
apparatus and systems of communication have abolished
every possibility of remoteness by bringing things closer
together. It is only because things have already been objectified and brought close that distance can subsequently appear
to be foreclosed by the intervention of radio, television, the
internet and so on.

For this reason, we can say that everything is and takes
place *in medias res*, meaning that we not only encounter

things as always and already mediated by objects but that this objective, middle position constitutes the baseline and starting point for our engagement with and understanding of things. In other words, mediation *comes first* and constitutes the primary condition in which we already find ourselves dealing with objects. Whatever remains outside the space and time of this prior objectification is, it seems, only able to be articulated and ascertained *via negativa* (Benso 2000: 82) which is perhaps the reason why Heidegger spills a considerable amount of ink telling us what things are not. There is, as we have already recognized in chapter 1, a clue to this insight in etymology. The word 'immediacy' is often understood and employed as the opposite of and even antidote for mediation. Despite this, the fact of the matter is that the word 'immediacy' is assembled by appending the negative prefix 'im-' to the word 'media', indicating that 'immediate' is the derived concept, fabricated by way of negation (*via negativa*) from 'mediation', which is the primary and positive term. Consequently, the immediate presentation of the thing is something that is only able to be articulated negatively from out of a prior encounter with the object of mediated representation. This is, one may recall, substantially similar to what Baudrillard identifies with the iconic phrase 'the precession of simulacra' (1983 [1981]: 2). The representation, 'the map' in Baudrillard's terms, is not derived from the territory. The order of precedence is reversed. It is the territory that is derived from the map.

3. *There is no 'golden age'*: Directly following from this, there is no privileged 'golden age', when things would have been immediately present as things. For Heidegger, the effort to think things as things outside the influence of objectification is not and should not be interpreted as some reactionary back-to-nature, New Age mysticism that celebrates some earlier time that would have been uncontaminated by the

objectifying influence of modern science, telecommunications media or technology. Although Heidegger often makes reference to the seemingly simple and direct experience of the Schwarzwald peasant, he does not endorse nor does he advocate naive romanticism. He is emphatic on this point:

> If things ever had already shown themselves *qua* things in their thingness, then the thing's thingness would have become manifest and would have laid claim to thought. In truth, however, the thing as thing remained proscribed, nil, and in that sense annihilated. This has happened and continues to happen so essentially that not only are things no longer admitted as things, but they have never yet at all been able to appear to thinking as things. (TT: 170–1)

The remoteness of the thing, the inability to think the thing as thing, is not some recent catastrophe as compared to some earlier epoch, when things were originally thought as things. Quite the contrary, things *have never been* thought as things and this fundamental withdrawing of things, what Heidegger will also refer to as the 'forgetting of Being', is something that has occurred from the beginning and is definitive of philosophical thinking as such. Consequently, there is, for Heidegger at least, no 'golden age' to go back to, to celebrate or to try to recover. Getting rid of all the appliances, apparatuses and encumbrances of mediated objectification will not deposit us once again in some pristine Garden of Eden, where things would have been experienced as things and exposed before us in their unclothed nakedness.

4. *Changing things*: As a result of this inability to return to (a non-existent) Eden, we are not and should not make the assumption that we could be the agents of change. The problem of objectification, or, if you like, the withdrawing of the thing as thing, is not fixed by simply shifting focus or

changing people's minds about things. 'A mere shift in attitude,' Heidegger writes,

> is powerless to bring about the advent of the thing as thing.
> Just as nothing that stands today as an object in the dis-
> tanceless can ever be simply switched over into a thing.
> Nor do things as things ever come about if we merely avoid
> objects and recollect former objects which perhaps were
> once on the way to becoming things and even to actually
> presencing as things. (TT: 182)

In other words, things are out of our hands. We cannot by
brute force, clever shiftings of attitude or strength of will
make things different by doing something that would transform what had been distanceless objects into a thing proper.
We are, as Heidegger describes it, 'powerless to bring about
the advent of the thing'.

In the next chapter, we explore how the analytical framework with which *Being and Time* investigates things is further
developed to deal with the status of things within heav-
ily industrialized societies in ways that are either implicitly
or explicitly relevant to any consideration of the forms of
media we now encounter. In this context, recognition of our
powerlessness 'to bring about the advent of the thing' is exacerbated by the detailed analysis in Heidegger's later work of
how things become yet further objectified within ever more
complex technological systems. It is important to note that
this does not equate with a submissive form of fatalism or
even nihilism – a criticism that has often been applied to
Heidegger's work. Rather, it is derived from the fact that the
objectification of things is neither recent nor optional; it is a
done deal(ing). It has always and already taken place.

For this reason, changing things is not in our power. It
is not a matter of something we decide to do or not do.

It is itself fated. It is already the fate of all things. It is as Heidegger will say, the 'destiny of Being' (EOP: 9). So the remaining question, 'the question that is,' as Heidegger writes in 'The Turning', 'seemingly always the most immediate one and the only urgent one, is "What shall we do?"'(TUR: 40). Heidegger is, at least in his consideration of 'The Thing', silent on this particular matter. The response, therefore, comes by way of the sequels – the three remaining Bremen Lectures and the published essays based on this material. It is perhaps most succinctly articulated by way of a short quotation from the German poet Friedrich Hölderlin, which serves as a kind of refrain throughout this material: 'But where the danger is/The saving power also grows' (TT: 40). For Heidegger, this is something that concerns the very essence of technology and it is taken up and examined in considerable detail in the highly influential essay 'The Question Concerning Technology' to which we now turn.

4

THE *DASIGN* OF MEDIA APPS
The Questions Concerning Technology

INTRODUCTION

One observes technology technologically. To be sure, this manner of observation corresponds to technology . . . But in so doing even technological judgments about technology never arrive at the essence of technology . . . Thus it changes nothing if one abhors technology as disaster or prizes it as the greatest advance of humankind and extols it as the redeemer of humanity. . . . Without risking the step of thinking that exposes our human essence to the essence of technology (not only to its manipulations and uses), one struggles through these conflicts from case to case, situation to situation.

BFL: 55

Heidegger's nostalgia for a *völkisch* past . . . constitutes a basic quality of his rhetoric and thought.

Ziolkowski 2001: 360

The first of the above excerpts is from Heidegger's essay 'The Danger' and acts like a manifesto for the major questions he wants to explore concerning technology. It also contains a key element of his approach explored in this chapter – his rejection of analyses that focus upon particular technologies at the expense of considering the essence of technology. This focus on the essence of technology is a pivotal point differentiating his analysis from those who criticize it, either for being too abstract, or for relying upon a *völkisch* (folksy) nostalgia – an unrealistic desire to return to a pre-technological idyll. In response to the view of Heidegger as an excessively abstract or nostalgic thinker, this chapter explores the manner with which he strives to understand the *essence* of technology in order to move beyond the sort of correct, but ultimately limited, case-by-case descriptions of individual types of technology. These descriptions tend to dominate Communication Studies but they leave the environment-defining nature of technology largely unexamined. A glib or dismissive rejection of the essential questions that Heidegger raises about technology's essence results in an inherently limited perspective – a perspective trapped in the unilluminated position of observing technology technologically.

In 1949, Heidegger gave a series of talks at the Bremen Club. Presented under the collective title of *Insight Into That Which Is*, they included pieces entitled 'Positionality', 'The Danger', 'The Turn' and 'The Framework', and these lectures formed the basis of the most significant of all Heidegger's writings on technology, 'The Question Concerning Technology' (1977 [1962]) (henceforth referred to as QCT). In QCT, Heidegger's distinction between truth and correctness previously addressed in chapter 2 once again comes to the fore. He begins QCT with the 'instrumental and anthropological definition of technology', the commonplace notion that technology is just a means to an end, and proceeds to ask 'who would ever deny that it is correct?' (QCT: 5) In opposition to this 'current conception', he draws upon the previously encountered notion of ἀλήθεια as unconcealment to open up another thinking of the essence of technology, namely that 'technology is no mere means ... It is the realm of revealing, i.e., of truth' (QCT: 12). As Dallmayr (1989: 91) points out, 'In Heidegger's treatment, *Wesen* [essence] means "to permeate" or "to be steadily present with" [*Anwesen*]', and in this seemingly abstruse philosophical nuance one can find an understanding of media that is based upon a critical investigation of how instrumentality permeates throughout society. This, we argue, is what sets Heidegger's analysis apart. The conventional focus upon the particularity of individual media instruments is ultimately much less revealing than an analysis of *instrumentality*'s ability to mediate our world.

Heidegger's later work can be characterized by what was described in chapter 1 as *die Kehre* (the turn) that, along with an increased focus on language, also marks a change from a concern with *doing* in his earlier work to one of *dwelling* and an increased interest in the *openness to Being*. This shift in emphasis enables a sustained level of attention to the problems of being in a technologically mediated world and provides an invaluable resource by which to understand the contemporary lived experience of mediated Being – the technological *environment* understood in its most instrumentally permeated, existential sense. It is in the Bremen Lectures and, most notably, QCT that Heidegger provides an extended analysis of how disclosure is framed or determined by technology's essence. Through Heidegger's analysis, we see how technology dominates not simply in terms of its omnipresence but, even more importantly, through the standardized mindset that it inculcates in its users *whatever piece of technology is used.* This insight is perhaps the most important and least understood of Heidegger's contributions to our understanding of media.

THE INSTRUMENTALITY OF INSTRUMENTS

The correct instrumental definition of technology still does not show us technology's essence. In order that we may arrive at this, or at least come close to it, we must seek the true by way of the correct. We must ask: What is the instrumental itself?

QCT: 6

Heidegger develops his questioning concerning technology by using a series of closely related concepts. *Positionality, requisitioning, enframement* and *standing reserve* are all examples of the sort of terms in his later essays that describe how technological systems determine the environment within which all objects and processes function, but here is the crucial point, *only in terms of those systems already designed to contain them* – a tautological situation whereby technological society's calculable complex fosters a cultural atmosphere in which calculating values dominate. 'Traditional metaphysics,' Francisco Rüdiger writes with reference to Heidegger's 'The Thing', 'was essentially poetical and expressed itself in an ontological thinking. Modern metaphysics is essentially mathematical and tries to express[es] itself in an anthropological thinking. Within it, calculus assumes a dominance or a first-rank significance over the mundane and/or divine proprieties of the things' (Rüdiger 2004: 76; see also Rüdiger 2006: 101). Rüdiger's distinction between these two types of metaphysics – 'traditional metaphysics' and 'modern metaphysics' – goes straight to the heart of the contrast between Heidegger's approach to instrumentality itself and objectivist theories like the mathematical model of communication that presuppose their own instrumentality. Thus, whereas the mathematical model instrumentalizes communication by making it nothing more than the transmission of quantifiable and calculable forms of data (hence the adjective 'mathematical'), Heidegger emphasizes the context or framing that makes this instrumental conceptualization possible in the first place.

In this context, *en-framing* is a key notion, which 'means the gathering together of that setting-upon which sets upon man, i.e., challenges him forth, to reveal the real, in the mode of ordering, as standing-reserve' (QCT: 20). Enframing has two main aspects – things become situated as, and thereby reduced to the status of, available objects and human beings themselves become part of this same process of objectification even as they are busy objectifying the world around themselves. The concepts of *enframing* and *standing reserve* therefore help to illuminate not only the manner in which entities are organized for technologically facilitated exploitation but also the mentality that both underlies and results from this calculable complex. Rather than encountering things as things, we come preconditioned to treat the world (and ourselves) as part of a standing reserve of preconditioned objects, or, as Heidegger expresses it: 'Enframing means that way of revealing which holds sway in the essence of modern technology and which is itself nothing technological' (QCT: 20).

Enframing and standing reserve hence relate to the particular mode of revealing, a challenging-forth, that occurs within modern technological environments and which Heidegger contrasts with the bringing-forth that takes place within *poiesis*. This Greek word, as noted previously, provides us with the root of the word 'poetry' but Heidegger deploys it more broadly in order to articulate an approach to things that is otherwise than what is possible within the standard, instrumentalist context. For Heidegger, however, what is important here is not the different instruments that are used, i.e. the hand tools of the traditional craftsman versus industrialized machines or even automated, computer controlled manufacturing systems. What matters is the way the worker comes to be related to the thing on which he works:

> One can object that today every village cabinetmaker works with machines . . . [Such objections fall] flat, because [they have] heard only half of what the discussion has to say about handicraft. The cabinetmaker's craft was chosen as an example, and it was presupposed thereby that it would not occur to anyone that through the choice of this example is the expectation announced that the condition of our planet could in the foreseeable future, or indeed ever, be changed back into a rustic idyll . . . However it was specifically noted that what maintains and sustains even this handicraft was not the mere manipulations of tools but the relatedness to wood. But where in the manipulations of the industrial worker is there any relatedness to such things as the shapes slumbering [*Gestalten*] in the wood? (WCT: 23)

This excerpt is significant for the manner in which it clearly repudiates the accusation of *völkisch* nostalgia that is frequently levelled at Heidegger's work. He clearly states that he is not anticipating a return to a rustic idyll whose time has passed. However, irrespective of whether current trends can be reversed or not, the qualitative difference between industrialized manufacture and tool-based handicraft is not the deciding issue. What matters is 'not the mere manipulations of tools' but how different technological systems frame a relationship to things. The advent of various virtual technologies (virtual memory/machines/realities/worlds/objects, etc.) of the digital age and its ubiquitous point-and-click interactivity means that Heidegger's rhetorical question about the industrial worker's ability to relate (or not) to the potential of 'such things as the shapes slumbering in the wood' faces the additional problem of an absence of even the ability/need to manipulate physical things at all.

THE TECHNOLOGICAL BOY SCOUT'S METAPHYSICAL SPHINX

> The abolition of the particular is turned insidiously into something particular. The desire for particularity has silted up while still at the stage of a need, and is reproduced on all sides by mass-culture, on the pattern of the comic strip. What was once called intellect is superseded by illustrations.
>
> Adorno 1991 [1951]: 141

In keeping with Adorno's typically catty denunciation of modern culture's widespread need for particular examples with which to illustrate general points, Heidegger's analysis of technology is frequently criticized for being too abstract and of little use for the close consideration of specific technologies. Thus Graham Harman (2010: 17) complains that, 'when he speaks of "technology," he has little to tell us about specific high-tech instruments. In both cases he is more concerned with a general ontology than with a theory of tools or technology'. Feenberg (1999: 187), meanwhile, bemoans the fact that 'unfortunately, Heidegger's argument is developed at such a high level of abstraction', whilst Heim (1993: 57) suggests that 'Heidegger speculated on an all-enframing *Gestell* [technological system], ominous and threatening, but an abstraction looming like a metaphysical sphinx, terrorizing thought with a puzzling lack of specificity.' Heim and others' criticism of Heidegger's excessive abstraction mis-takenly presupposes that instrumentality can (and should) be understood through an analysis of instruments; moreo-ver, whilst it is legitimate to question whether an ontological understanding is necessary or worthwhile in the first place, to accuse reasoning that is unapologetically ontological of being too abstract is akin to criticizing water for being too wet.

A short response to Harman's claim that Heidegger focuses upon developing 'a general ontology', rather than a theory of tools or technology, is therefore 'yes, guilty as charged'. Unsurprisingly, as a philosopher seeking to reha-bilitate the question of Being, Heidegger produces a general ontology. However, it is a profound mistake to assume from this that such a general ontology is automatically irrelevant to tools *or* technology. With his use of the conjunction 'or', Harman's criticism presupposes that an ontological theory of tools and technology could exist independently of each other which, from Heidegger's perspective, is not possible since both tools and technology participate in the disclosure of Being and would therefore need to be jointly explainable by any 'general ontology' worthy of the name. Criticisms that Heidegger's emphasis upon the systemic nature of modern technology makes his theory of little use for understanding the specific uses and potential of various individual gadgets is a correct one, however, such complaints can be seen as a symptom of the very technological mode of thinking that Heidegger's thought undermines, and therefore they miss a more important insight.

Additionally, the standard criticism that Heidegger's analysis of technology is somehow too abstract illustrates *in itself* a particular sort of (instru)mentality. A 'pragmatic anti-essentialism' that prides itself upon a sensitivity to the variety of technological experiences can only do so if

it reintroduces its own unacknowledged form of essential-
ism – the belief that all technologies are *essentially neutral*
prior to their use as means for freely chosen and humanly
defined ends. The desire for a more specifically useful theory
is, in itself, a revealing example of the conceptual inability/
unwillingness to make a distinction between an ontological understanding of how *things* are disclosed and how, by
contrast, technological *objects* disport themselves within an
overarching technological environment preconditioned for
the experience of objects rather than things.

Heidegger uses the term *positionality* to describe this cir-
cumscription of objects such that, paraphrasing Adorno,
they belong to a technological order even before they join
it. Failing to appreciate this distinction is what traps analysts
into viewing technology technologically. It is, for example,
what leads to direct (but mistaken) equivalences being made
between traditional crafts and 'new crafts' such as computer
programming. Heidegger clearly rejects this comparison,
arguing that objects produced by machines are 'essentially
different from handicraft activity, assuming that there is
still anything at all like craft production within positionality' (BFL: 34). Positionality thus describes, as we saw in
the previous chapter, the degraded ontological condition of
technological objects whose status as *things* has atrophied.

Again, Heidegger's argument receives backing from the
unlikely source of Adorno, as can be seen in this scathing
description of the typical amateur radio enthusiast[1]:

At twenty, he is still at the stage of a boy scout working on
complicated knots just to please his parents. This type is
held in high esteem in radio matters. He patiently builds
sets whose most important parts he must buy ready-made,
and scans the air for short-wave secrets, though there are
none. As a reader of Indian stories and travel books, he once

discovered unknown lands and cleared his path through the forest primeval. As radio ham, he becomes the discoverer of just those industrial products which are interested in being discovered by him. *He brings nothing home that would not be delivered to his house.* (Adorno 1991 [1938]: 54; emphasis added)

Although a staunch critic of Heidegger, Adorno's dismissal of the radio ham's faux-independence nevertheless constitutes a vivid depiction of the Heideggerian notion of positionality inherent to a specific media technology that derives its whole purpose from its place within a broader communicational system. Thus, although at first glance disorientatingly complex, *en-framing*'s definition as 'the gathering together of that setting-upon which sets upon man, i.e., challenges him forth, to reveal the real, in the mode of ordering, as standing-reserve' (QCT: 20) is vividly exemplified in Adorno's ham radio operator. The apparatus he patiently builds, in its turn, sets upon its maker in a series of depredations whereby the radio ham is reduced to the status of a boy scout demonstrating technical skill merely to gain parental recognition; his acts of construction only involve that which can be purchased ready-made; the secrets he seeks do not exist; the things he does discover were there all along; and, as a consequence of all these factors, he uncovers nothing new since he is only able to deliver that which was already there.

For Heidegger, therefore, a true understanding of mediated Being requires insight into its essential conditions/position, rather than accepting the 'correct' but ultimately unenlightening Boy Scout conceptualization of technology understood technologically:

Technology is not equivalent to the essence of technology. When we are seeking the essence of 'tree', we have to become aware that that which pervades every tree, as tree, is not itself a tree that can be encountered among all the other trees. Likewise, the essence of technology is by no means anything technological. Thus we shall never experience our relationship to the essence of technology so long as we merely conceive and push forward the technological, put up with it, or evade it. (QCT: 4)

Just as there is no one tree for which the word 'tree' fully corresponds, the essence of technology lies outside of any one particular artefact, and it *is by no means anything technological*. This counter-intuitive but explicit statement marks in the clearest possible terms the precise departure point between those who see a truth in Heidegger's ontology that has relevance for the essence of media and those who prefer to retain a correct focus upon the hi-tech excrescences of particular technological objects. Or as Heidegger puts it: 'Machine technology remains up to now the most visible outgrowth of the essence of modern technology' (AWP: 116). And now this mechanical technology has been superseded by its electronic, digital, virtual and nano-tech descendants.

A failure to see any fundamental difference between basic tools (e.g. hammers and chisels) and the use of artefacts that function within complex technological systems (e.g. computers, algorithms, networks, etc.) presupposes an instrumentalist understanding of technology (which is clearly similar to the instrumentalist theory of language explored in chapter 1) that endorses what Langdon Winner (1977: 27) calls *the myth of neutrality*. Neither good nor bad, technology's effects result from how we choose to use it. Heidegger's approach rejects the notion of technological neutrality, the exclusive agency of human subjectivity and a perceived need to focus upon specific technologies as self-evident sources of meaning. Like McLuhan, who argued that 'our conventional response to all media, namely that it is how they are used that counts, is the numb stance of the technological idiot' (1995: 18), Heidegger is unequivocal that technology is profoundly non-neutral: 'Everywhere we remain unfree and chained to technology, whether we passionately affirm or deny it. But we are delivered over to it in the worst possible way when we regard it as something neutral; for this conception of it, to which today we particularly like to do homage, makes us utterly blind to the essence of technology' (QCT: 4).

What makes Heidegger's question concerning technology so important for understanding the media is precisely the manner in which his philosophy deals with this essence of abstract, but nonetheless powerfully determining, tendencies that pervade *all* communications technologies. In this context, Heim's description of 'an abstraction looming like a metaphysical sphinx terrorizing thought with a puzzling lack of specificity' could be more usefully co-opted as an eloquent expression of the phenomenological experience of technology's (particularly media's) powerfully pervasive but often nebulous influence. Confronted by such nebulousness, Heidegger's concept of *positionality* enables us to obtain a better understanding of the full extent of the techno-logical (instru)mentality that comprises what Rüdiger calls 'modern metaphysics'.

THE MEDIA'S POSITION

The carpenter in the village does not complete a box for a corpse. The coffin is from the outset placed in a privileged spot of the farmhouse where the dead peasant still lingers. There, a coffin is still called a death-tree [*Totenbaum*]. The death of the deceased flourishes in it. This flourishing determines the house and farmstead, the ones who dwell there, their kin, and the neighborhood. Everything is otherwise in the motorized burial industry of the big city. Here no death-trees are produced.

BFL: 25

In caste societies, feudal or archaic, *cruel* societies, the signs are limited in number, and are not widely diffused, each one functions with its full value as interdiction, each is a reciprocal obligation between castes, clans, or persons. The signs are therefore anything but arbitrary. The arbitrary sign begins when, instead of linking two persons in an unbreakable reciprocity, the signifier starts referring back to the disenchanted world of the signified, a common denominator of the real world toward which no one has any obligation.

Baudrillard 1983 [1981]: 84–5

Surprisingly for someone with a *völkisch* reputation, the juxtaposition of the above two quotations demonstrates the close thematic similarity that exists between Heidegger's interpretations of the technological society and that of Baudrillard – a theorist frequently used as a shorthand reference for a distinctly un-*völkisch* and cynically postmodern portrayal of a society irredeemably suffused by simulations and the progenitor of that familiar tag-line from *The Matrix* trilogy, 'the desert of the real' (Baudrillard 1983 [1981]: 2). The first quotation comes from the second of Heidegger's Bremen Lectures, 'Positionality', and, as the essay's title conveys, here Heidegger is explicitly concerned with the situation of things – the way 'what is set here stands in the purview of what concernfully approaches us'. Words such as 'approaches', 'nearness', 'lingers', 'flourishes' all express a sense of positioning within either space or time that share Baudrillard's sense of 'reciprocal obligation'.

Heidegger contrasts the openness inherent to such

authentic positioning as the death-tree within a village with the unambiguously fixed sense of an objectified coffin 'merely finished' as part of the motorized burial industry. Similarly, in the second quotation taken from Baudrillard's *Simulations*, language itself is now finished, reduced as it is to a 'common denominator' in a 'disenchanted world of the signified'. 'Death-tree' expresses finality but by means of an almost oxymoronic term which emphasizes the fact that, although an inanimate thing, the wood that constitutes the coffin, like the corpse it now contains, previously lived. 'The death of the deceased flourishes in it' marks Heidegger's reintroduction of an enduring presence at the heart of death.

The coffin's setting in a village context re-acquaints us with the conception of 'setting', not in the sense of a static scene/tableau (or carpenter's table for that matter), but rather, 'setting' understood as a thing's placement in a situation in which the meaning of the thing and its surroundings are inextricably linked and mutually supporting. The coffin's status as a thing only truly makes sense when considered in position to the rural cottage, farmstead, inhabitants, relations and surrounding neighbours. In literature, a similar sentiment is contained within Miguel Delibes's 1950 classic Spanish countryside novel *El Camino* (The Road/Path/Way – the title supplying further resonance, given Heidegger's intention of 'building a way' to truth and the use of terms like *Holzwege* (*Off the Beaten Track*) and *Wegmarken* (*Pathmarks*) as the titles to two volumes of his collected essays). The reader encounters Delibes's village characters via nicknames generated from their enduring presence and biographical incidents as opposed to the proxies for identity more commonly used in cities – one's occupation and/or financial status.

Heidegger's use of the 'death-tree' to explain the distinction between 'what concernfully approaches us' is reinforced in QCT by his account of the Aristotelian *four causes* which he illustrates in relation to the making of a silver chalice. At the beginning of his example, Heidegger questions our basic understanding of causality by drawing upon the ancient Greek and Latin roots of the word. He points out that: '*Causa, casus*, belongs to the verb *cadere*, "to fall", and means that which brings it about that something falls out as a result in such and such a way' (QCT: 7). To this Latin connotation of open-endedness signally missing in the modern understanding premised upon a linearity of 'cause and effect', Heidegger then adds the further context of the Ancient Greek understanding whereby: 'What we call cause [*Ursache*] and the Romans call *causa* is called αἴτιον [*aition*] by the Greeks, that to which something else is indebted [*das, was ein anderes verschuldet*]. The four causes are the ways, all belonging at once to each other, of being responsible for something else' (QCT: 7).

The four causes referred to here are:

- *causa materialis* – the material or substance from which the chalice is fashioned, in this case silver;
- *causa formalis* – the form the chalice assumes by which we are able to recognize it as a chalice;
- *causa finalis* – the end or purpose for which the chalice is made in the first place, i.e. a religious service;
- *causa efficiens* – the making of the chalice in the most proficient or efficient fashion.

Heidegger argues that there has been a tendency to privilege the *causa efficiens* such that, even though it is only one of four, it has become the de facto standard from which we have come to judge all causality (QCT: 7). The significance of this is that it removes from our interaction with things the element of what Baudrillard conveys in terms of 'reciprocal obligation' and 'unbreakable reciprocity' and which Heidegger discusses in terms of co-responsibility and mutual indebtedness. Things whose full nature comes from a combination of concernfully related qualities are reduced, especially in the modern technological age, to the status of objects devoid of all except efficiency-orientated usage.

Whether Heidegger has nostalgic tendencies or not, his critics remain confronted by the stubborn fact that exponentially increased levels of technological mediation seem to introduce a qualitative change in human experience. Likewise, irrespective of whether it is possible to turn the historical clock back or not, recognition of this qualitative change remains important for understanding precisely what happens when what is called 'media' mediate. However, familiarity breeds consent, and we have a cultural tendency to uncritically accept linguistic commonplaces that conceal the essence of such qualitative changes. For example, in general usage, 'interactivity' has become largely synonymous with digital communication and information systems. There is little, if any, recognition of the conceptual depredation that needs to be inflicted upon traditionally understood forms of interaction for interactivity to become a standard phrase used so uncritically in a digital context. Similarly, the tendency to take the 'media' element of *media*tion for granted encapsulates the reason why Heidegger argues so consistently that we need to go back to essential questions concerning technology – for example, the deceptively simple concept of nearness.

MEDIATED NEARNESS

Man puts the longest of distances behind him in the shortest of time. He puts the greatest distances behind himself and thus puts everything before himself at the shortest range.

Yet this frantic abolition of all distance brings no nearness; for nearness does not consist in shortness of distance. What is least remote from us in point of distance, by virtue of its picture on film or its sound on radio, can remain far from us. What is incalculably far from us in point of distance can be near to us. Short distance is not in itself nearness. Nor is great distance remoteness.

TT: 163

In Heidegger's example, the death-tree 'is set here in nearness' so that it is encountered as a vividly felt part of communal life. By contrast, telecommunications media create a shrinking down of time and space where everything gets lumped together into uniform distancelessness (TT: 164). In terms initially not dissimilar to Heidegger's, Walter Benjamin explains in his seminal essay 'The Work of Art in the Age of Mechanical Reproduction' (1973 [1936]), that any traditional conception of 'aura' based upon the notion of presence at a unique point in space and time has been diminished. A keenly felt sense that the telecommunications systems of radio, film and television (distinctly twentieth-century examples that are entirely consistent with the time these individual thinkers lived and worked) herald the advent of unprecedented, qualitatively new experiences is thus not one that is unique to Heidegger. The very beginning of Benjamin's essay, for example, starts with an epigraph from Paul Valéry that states 'For the last twenty years neither matter nor space nor time has been what it was from time immemorial', and the essay proceeds as a sustained attempt to engage with the full implications of these remarkable changes. But this is not, we should point out, an insight or issue limited to mid-twentieth-century media technology. One can, for instance, see this line of reasoning at work in Marshall McLuhan's concept of the 'global village' (1995:

5), Paul Virilio's analysis of 'speed' (1997 [1995]), Bernard Stiegler's *Technics and Time*, vol. II (2009 [1996]), Pierre Lévy's *Cyberculture* (2001 [1997]) and Florian Rötzer's philosophical investigation of cyberspace (1998).

Rather than the implosive, shrinking effects that Heidegger describes, for Benjamin the experiential effects of modern representational media are explosive:

> Then came the film and burst this prison-world asunder by the dynamite of the tenth of a second, so that now, in the midst of its far-flung ruins and debris, we calmly and adventurously go traveling. With the close-up, space expands; with slow motion, movement is extended. The enlargement of a snapshot does not simply render more precise what in any case was visible, though unclear: it reveals entirely new structural formations of the subject . . . The camera introduces us to unconscious optics as does psychoanalysis to unconscious impulses. (Benjamin 1973 [1936]: 238–9)

In Benjamin's view, modern media technologies help to disclose revelatory new forms of nearness; for Heidegger, truth withdraws in the face of a surfeit of correct representations and the experience of nearness is much less transparent than it might appear to be. The proliferation of media, therefore, generates a technologically facilitated collapse of temporal delay and spatial distance but simultaneously inhibits our full appreciation of the precise nature of that implosion because: 'the frantic abolition of all distances brings no nearness; for nearness does not consist in shortness of distance' (TT: 163). In keeping with our repeated emphasis upon Heidegger's key role as a sustained questioner of some of our most basic assumptions, he uses his discussion of mediated time and space to ask a series of direct and probing questions: 'What is nearness if it fails to come about despite the reduction of the longest distances to the shortest intervals? What is nearness if it is even repelled by the restless abolition of distances? What is nearness if, along with its failure to appear, remoteness also remains absent?' (TT: 163–4).

This series of questions leads Heidegger to a key rhetorical question: 'Is not this merging of everything into the distanceless more unearthly than everything bursting apart?' (TT: 164). Heidegger's choice of 'bursting apart' resonates with Benjamin's 'burst this prison-world asunder,' but, and this is crucial, he asks us to consider the 'unearthly' nature of what is normally passed over due to the superficial impressiveness of media's implosive/explosive qualities. This is a concern explored elsewhere in the contemporaneous mass culture critiques of Adorno and Kracauer.

Whilst similar in terms to Heidegger's *das Man*, Kracauer discusses *Die Angestellten* (the salaried masses) and *Girltum* (girldom). In our own time, we have already seen how for Baudrillard, in a mediated world of the lowest common denominator, *signs* are uniform in their free-floating arbitrariness (think of the internationalized promiscuity of the Nike swoosh) and innately lack the sort of pressing obligation that is found in culturally grounded *symbols*.

This distanceless aspect of mass media culture is both what is most significant about it but also what appears most natural to it. Whilst Benjamin concentrates on the radically new vistas opened up to human perception, Heidegger, and a number of critical theorists who follow him (in both senses of the word, 'coming after Heidegger in temporal sequence' and 'following the lead of Heidegger's thinking'), ask us to reconsider the truly radical effect of telecommunications media – the fact that, rather than creating unprecedented experiences of a global village, media compress things into an unearthly sameness, which we unfortunately fail to appreciate fully.

MEDIA APPS: THE REQUISITIONING OF UNIFORM DISTANCELESSNESS

The standing reserve persists through a characteristic positioning. We name it requisitioning [*das Be-Stellen*, to beset with positioning].

BFL: 25

As the literal English translation 'here/there-being' indicates, *Da-sein* innately relates to positional presence, that is, being-in-the-world with other entities. We can see from the above excerpt, however, the manner in which Being is mediated through 'standing reserve', and the notion of an enduring presence is replaced with the persistence of *requisitioning*. This provides Heidegger with another term with which to describe what should now be a familiar theme: the reduction of a thing's place, rich with poietic possibilities, to the status of an object positioned within an order of systemic predestination – the distinctly non-poietic and challenged-forth nature of a standing reserve in which an object's mode of existence consists of 'applications' that, in actuality, have already been decided in advance. Despite his reputation for abstruse philosophizing, Heidegger's conceptualization of requisitioning readily applies itself to a contemporary mediascape dominated by the latest 'apps'. Given the currency the word now has with the advent of tablets, smartphones and similar devices, Heidegger uses the term 'application' with inadvertent prescience, and it clearly resonates with much more recent critiques of the unearthly uniformity introduced into human experience by contemporary media technologies.

In one of Baudrillard's final works, *The Intelligence of Evil* (2005 [2004]), the concept of 'integral reality' is used largely synonymously with Heidegger's notion of the standing reserve and its various associated terms (requisitioning, enframing, positioning, challenging-forth, etc.). Baudrillard's conceptualization of a 'totalitarian semiotic order' effectively describes how the requisitioning of physical objects in what Benjamin called 'the age of mechanical reproduction' expands pervasively and invasively to include abstract signs in a digital age. The terms Heidegger uses to characterize the essence of technology are re-presented in Baudrillard in the form of a distinction between production and seduction:

> From the discourse of labour to the discourse of sex . . . one finds the same ultimatum, that of pro-duction in the literal sense of the term. . . . To produce is to materialize by force what belongs to another order, that of the secret and of seduction. Seduction is, at all times and all places, opposed to production. Seduction removes something from the order of the visible, while production constructs everything in full view . . . Everything is to be produced, everything is to be legible, everything is to become real, visible, accountable . . . *this is the enterprise of our culture*, whose natural condition is obscene: a culture of monstration, of demonstration, of productive monstrosity. (Baudrillard 1990 [1979]: 34–5)

The unearthly experience of uniform distanceless identified by Heidegger is vividly portrayed by Baudrillard as producing a society of uncontrolled reality, a world of fractal simulations in which the difference between reality and its representations has broken down as we experience their irretrievable and mutual imbrication. *The Perfect Crime* (2002 [1995]) is the title Baudrillard gives to the (il)logical conclusion of the technology-facilitated requisitioning of reality. The crime is perfect because, if reality has been murdered, then, by definition, no trace of the crime is left behind. The result is an environment characterized as hyperreal – a mode of reality that is more real than the real itself, reaching a point at which 'the task of all media and information today is to produce this real, this extra real (interviews, live coverage, movies, TV-truth, etc.). There is too much of it; we fall into obscenity and pornography. As in pornography, a kind of zoom-in takes us too near the real, which never existed and only ever came into view *at a certain distance*' (Baudrillard 1983 [1978] :84).

What Heidegger describes as unearthly, Baudrillard views as pornographic or *ob*-scene – the distance necessary for a scene to be witnessed as a scene has been removed by the camera's relentless telephoto zoom. Like McLuhan, Baudrillard develops this theme of distancelessness using the myth of Narcissus.

> Bending over a pool of water, Narcissus quenches his thirst. His image is no longer 'other'; it is a surface that absorbs and seduces him, which he can approach but never pass beyond. For there is no beyond, just as there is no reflexive distance between him and his image. The mirror of water is not a surface of reflection, but of absorption. (Baudrillard 1990 [1979]: 67)

'Distancelessness' remains a kind of unifying thread in the work of Baudrillard, Benjamin, Heidegger and McLuhan, even if each thinker develops the concept in their own unique manner and idiom in order to grapple with its implications for the mediated experiences of media.

MEDIA CIRCUITS: THE CHAIN OF REQUISITIONING

What is ordered is always already and always only imposed upon to place another in the succession as its consequence.

The chain of requisitioning does not run out to anything; rather it only enters into its circuit.

BFL: 28

A circular construction where one presents the audience with what it wants, an integrated circuit of perpetual solicitation.

Baudrillard 1990 [1979]: 163

Throughout this book and this chapter, we have highlighted the positional nature of Heidegger's thinking:

* being-in-the-world as the basic state of *Dasein* (BT: 78);
* *logos* as 'the pure letting-lie-together-before of that which of itself comes to lie before us, in its lying there' (EGT: 66);
* enframing defined as 'the gathering together of that setting upon which sets upon man' (QCT: 20).

The media play a central role in this positionality by creating a society-wide condition of uniform distancelessness well-encapsulated in the title *One-Dimensional Man* (2002 [1964]), a book by Heidegger's student Herbert Marcuse. From a Heideggerian perspective, telecommunications media can be viewed as a 'chain of requisitioning' that produces a condition that persists rather than presences. This is a perspective that closely fits Baudrillard's notion of the media as a 'circular construction', an 'integrated circuit of perpetual solicitation' in which culturally grounded rich *symbols* are replaced by highly transmissible but ultimately empty *signs*. The question then arises as to the fate of *Dasein* in such an environment. The Frankfurt School critical theorists were scathing in their critique of the existentially deadening effects of the culture industry's mass media but, a comparison of their analysis with Heidegger's work not only further illustrates notions of enframing and challenging-forth but also raises a series of interesting questions regarding, *pace* Lenin, what is to be done in such a situation and whether it is either possible or necessarily desirable to seek to escape from the chain of requisitioning that results from today's pervasive manifestations of that chain.

The status of the work of art in the age of mechanical reproduction previously encountered in Benjamin's work offers particularly useful insights into some of these questions. For example, the potentially profound loss in our openness to Being caused by media is usefully summarized in the contrast Benjamin's colleague Kracauer makes between the artwork and a photograph:

> In order for history to present itself, the mere surface coherence offered by the photograph must be destroyed. For in the artwork the meaning of the object takes on spatial appearance, whereas in photography the spatial appearance is its meaning. The two spatial appearances – the 'natural' one and that of the object permeated by cognition – are not identical. By sacrificing the former for the sake of the latter, the artwork also negates the likeness achieved by photography. This likeness refers to the look of the object, which does not immediately divulge how it reveals itself to cognition; the artwork, however, conveys nothing but the transparency of the object. In so doing, it resembles a magic mirror which reflects those who consult it not as they appear but rather as they wish to be or as they fundamentally are. The artwork, too, disintegrates over time; but its meaning arises out of its crumbled elements, whereas photography merely stockpiles the elements. (Kracauer 1995 [1963]: 52)

In the artwork 'permeated by cognition', there is a bringing-forth of Being, whereas the photograph 'merely stockpiles the elements' and therefore more closely relates to Heidegger's concept of the standing reserve (*Bestand*) and all the implications of *setting upon* that ensue from it.

Faced with the mass media's undermining of traditional 'high' art, Adorno sought a free relationship to Being in the notion of autonomous art, art conceived as a realm of human endeavour that was insulated from the *causa efficiens* type of solicitation: 'In so far as a function may be predicated of works of art, it is the function of having no function' (Adorno 1997: 227). However, the possibility of there being an outside to a technologically determined disclosure of Being, an outside unconstrained by instrumentality-infused values, is much less clear from the work of Adorno's Frankfurt School associates Benjamin and Kracauer. In Benjamin's eyes, for example, the significance of the advent of photography and film is less about the technologies' status as art forms and much more about the extent to which these technological developments have shattered and made anachronistic traditional conceptions of art as a realm of freedom.

Meanwhile, in Kracauer's work we can find a simultaneous acknowledgement of media's enervating effect upon society and a denial that a solution can be found by rejecting or avoiding technological developments. In his essay 'The Hotel Lobby', Kracauer uses the eponymous space as a metaphor to convey mass culture's spatio-temporal shallowness and self-referentiality. He argues that: 'In spheres of lesser reality, consciousness of existence and of the authentic conditions dwindles away in the existential stream, and clouded sense becomes lost in the labyrinth of distorted events whose distortion it no longer perceives' (Kracauer 1995 [1963]: 173). Kracauer's concern that we no longer perceive the nature of distortion taking place shares with Heidegger's concept of *danger* the idea that a certain degree of freedom is lost if we fail to recognize (withdraw from) our technologically facilitated withdrawal from reality (withdrawal from withdrawal) but, just as Benjamin responded to the apparent loss of auratic art, both Kracauer and Heidegger also refuse to find pat answers in art's purportedly saving power.

NOSTALGIA FOR THE SAVING POWER OF ART

In his lecture 'The Provenance of Art and the Destination of Thought', delivered in Athens in 1967, Heidegger asks whether today, after two and a half thousand years, art is still under the demand that once ruled in Ancient Greece. His answer to that question is negative: art no longer stems from within the national boundaries of a people; it no longer enjoys the onto-historical role it once had, and which consisted in grounding and instituting a clearing of being.

de Beistegui 2005: 143–4

It is distinctly ironic that although, as we have previously seen, Heidegger is frequently accused of being nostalgic for a pre-lapsarian non-technologized existence, he is, nevertheless, remarkably anti-nostalgic in his rejection of a simple return to the sort of art known by the Greeks as a possible source of sanctuary from technology's depredations. There is a risk that we confuse the description of a technology-facilitated change in the disclosure to Being with an outright condemnation of that change. Likewise, Jonathan Sterne (2005: 220) argues that Benjamin's theorization of aura, has been misread. Benjamin (1973 [1936]) describes in detail how aura is removed from reality 'like water pumped from a sinking ship', but to interpret this as nostalgia for a lost quality of experience misses the crucial Heideggerian insight that any sense of nostalgia is only made possible as a result of the technological process itself. 'Precisely because authenticity is not reproducible, the intensive penetration of certain (mechanical) processes of reproduction was instrumental in differentiating and grading authenticity' (Benjamin 1969: 243). 'In this formulation,' Sterne writes, 'the very construct of aura is, by and large, retroactive [Žižek would say, "retroactively (presup)posited" (1991: 209)], something that is an artefact of reproducibility, rather than a side effect or an inherent quality of self-presence. Aura is the object of a nostalgia that accompanies reproduction' (Sterne 2005: 36).

Similarly, in QCT, Heidegger's use of *poiesis* to portray an openness to Being that is not present in modes of technological disclosure in which things are systemically pre-ordered (enframed, set upon, challenged-forth) can be misinterpreted. Despite identifying the qualitative difference between such examples as a peasant's relationship to nature compared to that of an engineer, Heidegger is not nostalgic. We cannot, as he emphasizes above, go back to an earlier time (i.e. ancient Greece) when pursuits like art provided the clearing of being because this is always already lost to us. In so far as there is a saving power in this situation, it is to be found in technology. Since technology encompasses everything, including art, the only 'way out' is by working through it. Just as Heidegger says of the 'circle of thinking' in *Being and Time*, the point is not to get outside the circle, but to work through it in the right way.

The temptation remains, however, when considering our relationship to technology, to afford art a privileged status. In a letter to Benjamin from 1936, Adorno memorably claimed with regard to the distinction between high and low art that 'both are torn halves of an integral freedom to which, however, they do not add up' (Adorno in Jameson 1980: 123). For his part, Kracauer argues that: 'while in the higher spheres the artist confirms a reality that grasps itself, in the lower regions his work becomes a harbinger of a manifold that utterly lacks any revelatory word' (Kracauer 1995 [1963]: 173). So 'Radio, telephotography, and so forth – each and every one of these outgrowths of rational fantasy aimlessly serves one single aim: the constitution of a depraved omnipresence within *calculable dimensions*' (70; emphasis added).

Although Kracauer's depiction of 'calculable dimensions' resonates strongly with Heidegger's 'calculable complex' and his assessment of 'the lower regions' reads as a cultural manifestation of Heidegger's concepts of enframing, it is, nevertheless, a mistake to conclude from this critical account of mass culture that ready answers to the perceived problems of the mass media are to be found in a realm of high art somehow lying outside technology's reach:

> The stimulations of the senses succeed one another with such rapidity that there is no room left between them for even the slightest contemplation. Like *life buoys*, the refractions of the spotlight and the musical accompaniment keep the spectator above water. The penchant for distraction demands and finds an answer in the display of pure externality; hence the irrefutable tendency ... to turn all forms of entertainment into revues and ... the increasing number of illustrations in the daily press ... This emphasis upon the external has the advantage of being *sincere*. It is not externality that poses a threat to truth. Truth is threatened only by the naïve affirmation of cultural values that have become unreal and by the careless misuse of concepts such as personality, inwardness, tragedy, and so on – terms that in themselves certainly refer to lofty ideas but that have lost much of their scope along with their supporting foundations, due to social changes ... They claim the status of

high art while actually rehearsing anachronistic forms
that evade the pressing needs of our time. (Kracauer 1995
[1963]: 326)

For Benjamin, Kracauer and Heidegger, the saving power
of truth cannot be found in attempts to ignore or avoid
contemporary technological developments with the naive re-
affirmation of outmoded concepts based upon an idealized
history of art.

For Kracauer, when confronted by the systematized
banalities of what he termed the *mass ornament*, the pressing concerns of our time require more not less development
so that: 'the problem is not that ratio^2 has gone too far but
that it has advanced too little and that capitalism "ration-
alizes not too much, but rather too *little*"' (Kracauer 1995
[1963]: 17). In practical media terms, this means that: 'the
path leads directly through the center of the mass ornament,
not away from it' (19). Whilst a mass media society already
has no meaning and 'the contours of such a society emerge
in the illustrated journals' (16), the search for meaning
involves more not less media. Thus, in terms of achieving what Kracauer calls a *liberated consciousness* (two terms
that, we should point out, Heidegger deliberately does not
employ because of their heavy metaphysical baggage), 'the
turn to photography is the *go-for-broke game* of history' (61).
Kracauer and Benjamin's observations do more than just
offer interesting insights into the early cultural conditions
of mass media society. Their chronicling of the industrially
motivated fragmentation of existence helps to illustrate the
relevance of Heidegger's project for an understanding of
media (and this is true even in situations where there is considerable disagreement between these thinkers with regard to
terminology, method of analysis and outcomes). Thus, when
in his 1925 essay 'Travel and Dance' Kracauer observes that:

'The manner in which special spatio-temporal events are currently being savored to the hilt is abundant confirmation that what is at stake in this very enjoyment is a distortion of an increasingly unavailable real existence' (Kracauer 1995 [1963]: 72), his words could just as easily be applied to the format of reality television, which can be viewed, in Heidegger's terms, as a relatively recent manifestation of the age of the world picture.

DASIGN: THE AGE OF THE WORLD PICTURE

Mankind, which was in the age of Homer an object of contemplation for the Olympian gods, has now become one for itself. Its self-alienation has reached such a degree that it can experience its own destruction as an aesthetic pleasure of the first order.

Benjamin 1973 [1936]: 242

With the word 'picture' we think first of all of a copy of something. Accordingly, the world picture would be a painting, so to speak, of what is a whole. But 'world picture' means more than this. We mean by it the world itself, the world as such, what is, in its entirety, just as it is normative and binding for us. 'Picture' here does not mean some imitation, but rather what sounds forth in the colloquial expression, 'We get the picture concerning something.'

AWP: 129

Like McLuhan and Baudrillard's previously cited reference to Narcissus, the above quotation highlights the manner in which, in a technological age, human contemplation narrows towards the self-absorbed. We use the term *Dasign* to help convey the particular importance of the contribution made by the media as the latter-day culmination of technology's historical enervation of *Dasein*.[3] In Heidegger's 'The Age of the World Picture', he explores this increasingly subjectivized mode of human experience. In particular, he uses the idea of 'picture' not to describe representational imitation but, rather, the mindset required for 'getting the picture'. Building on chapter 2's exploration of the historical dominance of the correspondence theory of truth, Heidegger's notion of *picture* usefully supplements the notion of literal depiction with the more abstract conceptualization of the disclosing nature of representational activity itself rather than just individual representations (much in the same way he explored the essence of instrumentality rather than just instruments).

In terms of the enframing-related concepts explored throughout this chapter, Heidegger's account of the 'world picture' (what we term *Dasign*) offers key insights into how the act of representation itself is challenged-forth and also the crucial recursive role this plays in the picturing of a world ripe for challenging-forth (the 'chain of requisitioning'). As before, Heidegger's back-to-basics approach starts with the Ancient Greeks. He distinguishes between the original Greek concept of *apprehending* and our modern notion of *representing*, which he argues is something quite different: 'To represent [*Vor-stellen*] means to bring what is present at hand [das *Vor-handene*] before oneself as something standing over against, to relate it to oneself, to the one representing it, and to force it back into this relationship to oneself as the normative realm. Wherever this happens, man "gets into the picture" in precedence over whatever is' (QCT: 131). The final sentence spells out the consequence of representation coming to replace apprehending – 'being in the picture' takes precedence over Being. By 'picture', however, Heidegger does not mean any particular image that would be placed before us.

> Where the world becomes picture, what is, in its entirety,
> is juxtaposed as that for which man is prepared and which,
> correspondingly, he therefore intends to bring before him-
> self and have before himself, and consequently intends in
> a decisive sense to set in place before himself ... Hence
> world picture, when understood essentially, does not mean
> a picture of the world but the world conceived and grasped
> as picture. (QCT: 129)

Thus here, in Heidegger's later work, we find a development
of his earlier treatment in *Being and Time* of the true nature
of equipment. Combining the two analyses together, it can
be seen how the roots of the media's tautologous circuit of
consequences lie in the ready-to-hand (*Zuhandenheit*) nature
of the instrument.

Simply focusing upon individual pieces of technology,
as we have seen critics of Heidegger proposing, brings us
no nearer to understanding readiness-to-hand, which is not
something manifest in the external appearance of things or
discovered by closely observing them (BT: 98). Like an air-
plane sitting on the runway (an example used in QCT), what
makes our dealings with technological things so qualitatively
different is the way in which they are preconditioned to be
part of an overarching project so that the objects positioned
within that system seamlessly 'subordinate themselves to the
manifold assignments of the "in-order-to"' (BT: 98). This
is the essential truth underlying McLuhan's aphorism, 'the
medium is the message', or, expressed in Heidegger's terms:
'the work bears with it that referential totality within which
the equipment is encountered' (BT: 99). For our media-
specific purposes, the crucial phrase here is the 'referential
totality' – the media's unobtrusive environment-defining
nature or the world picture that it frames. In this way, the
mode of work/communication is presupposed before the act

of communication itself – the effect of the technical form displaces the conceptual affect to the extent that the referential totality comes to constitute our notion of reality itself (BT: 106) in a manner that Guy Debord (1970 [1967]) later came to discuss in terms of 'The Society of the Spectacle'.

Dasign helps to convey the sense of the particular contribution to *existence* (*Dasein*) made by designs and signs that goes beyond the definite physicality of an object. Heidegger argues that, compared to concernful dealings with things (remember the carpenter's recognition of shapes slumbering in the wood), our encounter with systems of equipment is much more 'indefinite', even at close quarters. Although seemingly abstract, signs (whether linguistic in the form of spoken or written language, iconic in the manner of images and pictures or technical in terms of the underlying code of digital computers) serve to mediate, orientate and anchor our 'concernful dealings' not with specific artefacts, but with much more amorphous (but no less powerful) environments suffused with the quality of being ready-to-hand.

For Heidegger, the tendency to see signs as vehicles of indication is misleading. In his view, a sign is not one thing that refers to another thing. Instead, it is a piece of equipment that reveals a totality of equipment in such a way that the general character of the ready-to-hand is made apparent. It is, in other words, the way the ready-to-hand 'announces itself' to our 'circumspection' (BT: 110). Heidegger uses the term *circumspection* here in a markedly different fashion to its normal connotation of a careful consideration of context and possible consequences. For Heidegger, the term describes the naturalized manner in which we are oriented towards the in-order-to purpose of equipment rather than any specific thing. Equipment thus works as a referential totality and signs function within that totality to constitute our world (as) picture.

CONCLUSION

The threat to man does not come in the first instance from
the potentially lethal machines and apparatus of technology.
The actual threat has already affected man in his essence.
The rule of Enframing threatens man with the possibility
that it could be denied to him to enter into a more original
revealing and hence experience the call of a more primordial truth. Thus, where Enframing reigns, there is danger in
the highest sense. 'But where danger is, grows/The saving
power also.'

QCT: 28

We have seen in this chapter how Heidegger's importance
for understanding the media resides in his relentless inter-
rogation of the seemingly obvious in order to show how that
obviousness belies various unearthly qualities that reduce
things to a self-referential circuit of requisitioned applications. It is his 'pious' devotion to questioning the customary
understanding of technology, and the series of neutral operational assumptions it presupposes, that makes Heidegger's
analysis so useful for understanding a media environment
whose processes are routinely taken for granted because
they appear in such highly naturalized forms of representation. Thus, it is Heidegger's willingness to question the
very nature of instrumentality itself that lays the essential
groundwork for his subsequent examination of how media
technology embodies instrumentality and thereby effort-
lessly exerts its influence to create Baudrillard's previously
cited 'disenchanted world of the signifier'. Lazily dismissed
for his *völkisch* nostalgia, Heidegger's question concerning
technology raises the most contemporary of questions: What
happens when we are no longer tied together by 'unbreakable bonds of reciprocity'? How does one live authentically

in a world 'toward which no one has any obligation' and in which we increasingly only encounter ourselves in various enframed forms – the challenged-forth realm of *Dasign*?

In the end, Heidegger's *The Question Concerning Technology* does not supply us with prefabricated answers or easily formulated solutions. The outcome is more carefully structured and articulated. His objective, as indicated by the essay's title, is to bring technology into question, to make it questionable, and to demonstrate how the questioning concerning technology is already a questioning that proceeds from and is the concern of technology. Heidegger, therefore, does not (and quite deliberately so) answer the question concerning technology *for* us. Instead, he invites us into the task of questioning. This is not, despite initial appearances, something of a cop-out. It is a long-standing and venerable tradition in philosophy, which values learning how to ask the right questions over and against providing neatly wrapped up solutions that often do little more than reproduce the problems they were designed to resolve. In this and the previous chapters, we have shown the value of using Heidegger's form of ontological analysis to question not the correct functioning of particular media, but rather how the functioning of particular media can blind us to that functioning's true significance – the subject of our concluding thoughts . . .

CONCLUSION

There is Nothing Outside Technology

When the doors are barricaded, it is doubly important that thought not be interrupted.

Adorno 1991 [1969]: 200

Perhaps the only remaining attitude is one of waiting. By committing oneself to waiting ... One waits, and one's waiting is a *hesitant openness*, albeit of a sort that is difficult to explain.

Kracauer: 1995 [1963]: 138

This conclusion's subheading summarizes our interpretation of Heidegger's contribution to contemporary cultural theory. Like Derrida's *il n'y a pas de hors-texte* and Žižek's insistence that ideology is an inescapable part of the social condition, Heidegger's thinking suggests that it is precisely when we are faced with apparent necessity that we should question things most energetically. Having said this, there are few answers in the preceding pages. Heidegger eschews the excitement of neophile commentators who find endlessly exciting possibilities for human liberation in each new media development and, instead, he takes us back to the essence of technology. In an age when the doors of abstract thinking are besieged by media-friendly sound bites, 140-character tweets, and a general atmosphere of unreflexive, celebratory technological endorsement, Heidegger's stubbornly ontological approach both fits Adorno's insistence on the importance of uninterrupted thought and also gives voice to Kracauer's otherwise difficult-to-explain *hesitant openness*.

There is a distinction to be made between the idea that a situation is unavoidable and the subsequent conclusion that, because it is unavoidable, it is not worth reflecting upon. Similarly, throughout this book, we have seen that, whilst technology is indeed pervasive and ubiquitous and an essential component of how human beings come to experience the world, it is a false conceptual step to then conclude that technology is merely a neutral medium through which we encounter things. The technological condition may be inescapable, but recognition of this fact does not absolve us from questioning the implications of that fact and remaining open to and critical of the nature of our ongoing relationship with it – *an inescapable ontological condition is not the same as an inevitable phenomenological fact.*

In keeping with Heidegger's ontological approach, a constant emphasis in each chapter of this book has therefore been the need to reflect upon the structures that shape the disclosure of Being rather than just the individual manifestations of being. We have consistently shown how, from a Heideggerian perspective, to understand fully how media mediate, one needs to understand the relationship of a medium to its wider context. And various aspects of that context were addressed in successive chapters:

1 Language as a meta-medium – not just how we speak, but more importantly, how we are spoken.

2 The difference between *correctness* and *truth* – the common subordination of truthful revealing to the mere correctness of representation.

3 Things as entities situated in wider environments – the degree to which our experience of reality is objectified in advance.

4 How all these elements culminate in the structuring effects of technological systems – technology as that which constitutes the context for the revealing of things.

In terms of language and truth, in this book we have used phrases like 'essential questions ... about essence' and 'observing technology technologically'. This represents more than just a desire to ape Heidegger's mode of expression. The apparently tautological tone is instead a direct attempt to convey a sense of the manner in which Heidegger seeks a true understanding of technological processes by creating, through language, enough reflexive distance from those processes to avoid being unreflexively conditioned by them. Undaunted by dealing with the reality of abstractness, we have shown how Heidegger's mode of analysis is particularly useful for understanding the amorphously powerful nature of today's media environment. It meets a need for an understanding that goes well beyond case studies of any one particular gadget or communications device, or, most misguidedly of all, the notion that technology is essentially neutral.

In the previous chapters, we have consistently illustrated how, because their basic purpose is to mediate, media technologies are indeed frequently mistakenly viewed as neutral vehicles of phenomenological experience. This is true even in those disciplines like Media and Communication Studies that should be better equipped to reflect fully upon the implications of technology's more nuanced qualities. Heidegger's questions concerning technology relentlessly probe fundamental assumptions in order to devise a conceptual path out of the conventional. Most crucially, rather than concentrate upon the nature of technological instruments, this path leads us to a questioning of what constitutes instrumentality itself. This willingness to engage with the abstract tends to be misrepresented as a form of irredeemably inaccessible, non-pragmatic thought. Heidegger's thought, however, is anything but an other-worldly abstraction. Properly understood, it actually conceptualizes the relationship between the abstract and the particular by being pragmatic about πράγματα (things) in ways that, ironically, self-styled conceptual pragmatists are unable to match.

Our summary of the challenge offered by Heidegger's work to this arguably incomplete (mis)understanding of the media can be expressed in the form of three related equations. Fully aware of the irony that such equations are inevitably part of the 'calculable complex' we have critically interrogated, so acknowledged, they nevertheless help to encapsulate and reinforce the key elements and implications of Heidegger's indefatigable questioning of the technological enclosure of modern metaphysics explored in the previous chapters.

Equation 1
$$t = r = m$$

Technology, understood according to the standard instrumentalist and anthropological characterization (**t**), is equivalent, or at least substantially similar, to what Heidegger calls the 'ready-to-hand' (**r**) as it is developed and characterized in *Being and Time*. Both of these elements are understood as 'means to a humanly designated end' such that they are, quite literally, media (m) – a means or medium. This means that, for Heidegger, virtually everything is *media* and like the work of Marshall McLuhan, this conceptualization of 'media' is general and abstract, covering any and all aspects of the 'extensions of man'. But whereas McLuhan understands 'extension' as a kind of a posteriori appendage or prosthesis added onto human faculties, Heidegger goes one step further, characterizing 'extension' as the way that *Dasein* is always and already projected or extended into *concernful dealings* out of which things as technological objects come to be used and encountered.

'The media' is therefore not one technological object or complex of objects that is ready-to-hand among others, instead, it comprises the very ontological structure by which technological objects are encountered as such. This is why, despite not spending much of his time analysing 'the media', Heidegger's work plays such an important role in our understanding of the nature of its very pervasiveness. Rather than constituting an esoteric and excessively metaphysical outlook irrelevant to cutting-edge media developments (which is how Heidegger's work appears to have been typically treated by Communication Studies), his relentless questioning of apparently abstract and seemingly irrelevant notions of Being is in fact exactly what understanding the media requires. Heidegger's theorizing permits us to see what would otherwise be too close to us to recognize properly – the problem faced by McLuhan's fish and the sort of shifting of perspective Žižek describes in terms of *The Parallax View* (2006b).

In being everything (or, better stated, in articulating the being of everything), media comprise, as Heidegger demonstrates, the general condition of things – or more precisely stated, all things that are recognized and confronted by us as objects. This leads to:

Equation 2
$$t \neq T$$

The conventional understanding of technology (t) as the material artefacts and instruments with which we routinely interact, is, as Heidegger emphatically points out, correct. By this he means that it corresponds to our everyday conceptualization and experience of how technology appears, how it functions and how we come to evaluate it. This understanding of technology provides a benchmark that works. In fact, we could say that the instrumental definition of technology has been instrumental for us (human beings) to explain technology. But in being *correct*, or what Heidegger terms ὀρθότης following his reading of Plato's 'Allegory of the Cave', this formulation is not necessarily *true*. That is, it does not reveal (ἀλήθεια) the truth of technology in its essence (which we represent with the capital letter **T**). Consequently, technology, understood according to the standard instrumental and anthropological characterization (**t**) (and therefore media (**m**) following from the first equation), is not the same as technology in its essence (**T**). There is a significant difference between the entirely correct understanding of technology as an instrument of human action and involvement and the true essence of technology, which is, as Heidegger reminds us 'nothing technological'. This leaves us with one important question: What is **T**? What is the essence of Technology?

Equation 3
$$T = \tau + \lambda$$

An indication of the value or significance of **T** can be found in the word's etymology. 'Technology' is a compound of the Greek words τέχνη [*techne*] and λόγος [*logos*], that originary dimension of language (or what Heidegger had called *Rede* or discourse in the text of *Being and Time*). Consequently, we

can say that the essence of technology (**T**) can be found in
the sum of what is thought under the term *techne* (τ) and *logos*
(λ). Under 'technology', the *logos* – the originary dimension
of language that lays open the way to the being of things –
is accommodated to and regulated by *techne*, a word which
denotes not only that kind of making by way of the technical
arts but also the art of such technique.

Formulated in this fashion, technology for Heidegger
is not some external threat that comes from outside and
elsewhere. It does not appear, as is so often the case in contemporary science fiction, as terrifying robots and lethal
machines invading from another time or place. Instead, technology is already part and parcel of the logic (*logos*) by which
the world we already occupy – the picture of the world as we
perceive and know it – comes to be framed and made available and visible to us. For this reason, we cannot simply do
without technology. There is, to repeat once again Derrida's
provocation, nothing outside the technical order. There is
no place, position, or stance outside this particular logic
of enclosure or framing. What finally matters, then, is not
some ultimatum concerning media technology – a seemingly final and decisive either/or that opposes the modern
technological world-view to some romantic notion of a pre-
modern rustic idyll. This is not only a false dichotomy but
also a bogus choice portrayed by Heidegger's detractors as a
substitute for actually engaging with the implications of his
ontological analysis.

HEIDEGGER'S TRUTH REVISITED

Michael Heim's description of the consequences of the
reduction of truth to correspondence was previously cited in
chapter 2 but it is worth mentioning again in the light of this
book as a whole in order to re-emphasize the particular role

CONCLUSION 167

played by the media in the displacement of truth's disclosing power. 'Once the truth of being becomes equated with the light of unchanging intelligibility,' Heim (1993: 68) points out, 'the nature of truth shifts', and it shifts from 'truth as a process of disclosure' to truth understood as correctness – 'the ability of statements to reflect or refer reliably to entities'. This explains the sentiment behind Heidegger's counter-intuitive and discombobulating claim that we first presented in our Introduction 'making itself intelligible is the suicide of philosophy'. This is a deeply unfashionable position to hold in intellectually egalitarian times dominated by the values of reality TV and social media, for which seeing is believing, or, to repeat Gregory's resonant wording: 'intelligibility involves a uniform accessibility for the inauthentic anybody of an age marked by thoughtlessness' (Gregory 2007: 57).

The ultimate worth of Heidegger's undeniably difficult to understand content and mode of expression is the manner with which sustained engagement rewards the reader with a perspective from which conventional thoughtlessness about technology can be better appreciated for what it *truly* is. The theoretical distinction Heidegger makes between the terms 'correct' and 'true' and the accompanying suggestion that what is true may become hidden due to an over-abundance of the correct, however, also applies to the reception of Heidegger's own work. There are various correct appreciations that emphasize how his unconventionality can create a confusing read. But, as with the falsely presented dichotomy between rustic idyll and hi-tech society, this sort of appreciation frequently serves to deflect or displace a more important truth – the challenging new perspectives that are opened up when we apply his efforts and concerns to media.

Heidegger's questioning of truth, therefore, supplies four very useful and revealing insights that effectively challenge,

if not completely rewrite, the rules of media's game of
mediation:

• Heidegger explains the theory of truth that is already
  assumed and operationalized by media theory and practice. He not only describes the 'correspondence theory of
  truth' but locates the development of this conceptualization within the history of western thought.
• Heidegger submits this default setting to a thorough
  critical examination. He does this not because the usual
  way of doing things has been somehow wrong or inappropriate but because 'correspondence' cannot provide
  a satisfactory account of its own theoretical perspective.
  In particular, Heidegger demonstrates how correspondence and the correctness of representation – in either its
  idealist or realist form – needs and requires a prior disclosure of being in order to have something against which to
  compare representations and make evaluations about the
  truth or falsity of what is represented.
• To respond to this problem, Heidegger recovers a more
  original account of truth, one that is prior to correspondence in both historical sequence and conceptual status.
  This alternative is found in the ancient Greek word
  ἀλήθεια (*aletheia*) and uncovers truth as an original *unconcealing* from which correspondence is eventually derived
  as a kind of secondary application.
• Heidegger assigns the work of unconcealing to λόγος
  (*logos*), another Greek word that is translated by a number
  of related concepts: speech, language, logic, reason. In
  this way, he reconfigures the assumed relationship situated between words (and other forms of representation)
  and things: media and the means of representation are
  not merely instruments of communication or secondary
  phenomena that relate information about entities that

are already 'out there'; rather, they are direct and active participants in revealing the being of those things that we subsequently think they merely represent.

What ultimately matters from the combined import of these four points is how we, we who already find ourselves within the horizon of technology, come to dwell within our unavoidable enclosure by technology. How, in other words, one comes to occupy a place and time *in media(s) res*. Most importantly of all, Heidegger asks us to consider how we should understand and contend with the danger of this circumstance and what might save us.

THE SAVING POWER OF HEIDEGGER'S MEDIA THEORY

Could it be that the fine arts are called to poetic revealing? Could it be that revealing lays claim to the arts more primordially, so that they for their part may expressly foster the growth of the saving power, may awaken and found anew our look into that which grants and our trust in it? Whether art may be granted this highest possibility of its essence in the midst of the extreme danger, no one can tell. Yet we can be astounded. Before what? Before this other possibility: that the frenziedness of technology may entrench itself everywhere to such an extent that someday, throughout everything technological, the essence of technology may come to presence in the coming-to-pass of truth.

QCT: 35

With typical philosophical gutsiness, Heidegger throws us a curve ball with his counter-intuitive claim that, rather than seeking to escape technology's challenge in modes of Being such as art, it is in the midst of technology's frenziedness that we may find the most open response to its revealing essence. In the end, Heidegger's questions concerning technology do not supply us with prefabricated answers or easily formulated solutions. The outcome is more carefully structured and articulated. His objective, as indicated by the title of his most famous essay on this matter, is to bring technology into question. Heidegger, therefore, does not answer the question concerning technology. Instead, he involves us in the important work of questioning, which is the philosophical task par excellence. To reassert the point made at the very beginning of this book: 'There are,' as Žižek (2006a: 137) describes it, 'not only true or false solutions, there are also false questions. The task of philosophy is not to provide answers or solutions, but to submit to critical analysis the questions themselves, to make us see how the very way we perceive a problem is an obstacle to its solution.'

This is the truth behind Heidegger's rejection of a naive faith in the saving power of fine art and his claim that 'the closer we come to the danger, the more brightly do the ways into the saving power begin to shine' (QCT: 35). Thus, despite being largely ignored by Media and Communication Studies and despite his Nazi associations providing an immediate justification for dismissing Heidegger *tout court*, his work stubbornly persists in challenging the pervasively conventional and uncritical forms in which we routinely accept, rather than fundamentally question, the media that mediate Being. This is the reason why Heidegger ends 'The Question Concerning Technology' not with an answer, but with the statement that has served as this book's epigraph, but more importantly, its guiding thread throughout: 'questioning is the piety of thought' (QCT: 35).

NOTES

Introduction

1 The plessor is the small hammer-like medical instrument used by physicians on the patella tendon just below the knee in order to test the reflex response of a patient.

Chapter 1 We Need to Talk About Media

1 The assumed primacy of language in general and speech in particular has a long tradition in western thought. This is what Jacques Derrida has called and sought to investigate under the term logocentrism. 'If for Aristotle,' Derrida writes in *Of Grammatology* (1976 [1967]: 11), 'spoken words (*ta en te phone*) are the symbols of mental experience (*pathemata tes psyches*) and written words are the symbols of spoken words (*De interpretatione*, 1, 16a, 3) it is because the voice, producer of the first symbols, has a relationship of essential and immediate proximity with the mind. Producer of the first signifier, it is not just a simple signifier among others. It signifies "mental experiences"

which themselves reflect or mirror things by natural resemblance.' According to Derrida, this logocentrism pervades western philosophy up to and including the work of Heidegger.

2 Why, one might reasonably ask, does Heidegger decide to use the term *Rede*, when this word, especially when it is translated as 'talk', seems to be less 'dignified' than something like 'language', which is, at least since the 'linguistic turn' instituted during the mid-twentieth century, a kind of privileged philosophical concept? The answer to this question can be found in an ancient Greek word that has special significance for Heidegger – λόγος or logos as transliterated into more familiar Latin characters. This word, as Heidegger correctly points out, has been typically translated by the terms 'logic', 'reason', 'rationality' and 'word' (as we read, for example, at the beginning of the Gospel of St. John, 'In the beginning was the Word [*logos*]'). For Heidegger, what the ancient Greeks thought and tried to express by this word – this word that literally means word – was a primordial disclosure of being, what Heidegger (EGT: 66) will later characterize as 'the pure letting-lie-together-before of that which of itself comes to lie before us, in its lying there'. Heidegger calls this original disclosure *Rede*, because this German word resembles, in both its material form and etymology, the Latin word 'Ratio', which is one of the standard translations of logos throughout the history of philosophy. In chapter 4, the full significance of Ratio is expanded upon as we explore it, amongst other things, in terms of how the original conception of Ratio is radically altered so that its ontological role in the unconcealment of Being is reduced to its status as a reflection of the standardized nature of mass culture (Ratio, for example, is a key concept in Siegfried Kracauer's critique of industrialized culture in *The Mass Ornament*).

3 This phrase is directly lifted from a subheading that Heidegger had used in his notes for the 1939 graduate seminar, *On the Essence of Language* (OEL: 27).

4 Elsewhere, namely in 'The Way to Language' (WTL), Heidegger will distinguish originary language from ordinary language by calling the former 'saying', or *Sagen*.

5 For Heidegger, these meta-linguistic efforts, mainly evident in the analytic tradition, do not escape language and linguistics but constitute its ultimate realization: 'The metalinguistic treatment of language that is now coming to predominance in the Anglo-Saxon countries, the production of "metalanguages," is surely not the liberation from linguistics, but rather its perfect reification' (BFL: 153).

Chapter 2 Mediated Truth

1 This paradox whereby the obvious can remain hidden because it is too obvious is memorably portrayed in Edgar Allen Poe's story 'The Purloined Letter', in which the much sought-after eponymous letter turns out to be residing in full view on a noticeboard.

2 This choice of example is not accidental. It is borrowed from and makes reference to an internet prank that was seeded by Stephen Colbert of Comedy Central's *The Colbert Report*. In an episode from July of 2006, Colbert introduced his readers to the word 'wikiality'. This neologism was, as Colbert explained, derived from the experience and features of the online encyclopedia Wikipedia, where 'any user can change any entry, and if enough users agree with them, it becomes true' (Comedy Central 2006). As proof of concept, Colbert urged his viewers to go to Wikipedia and deliberately manipulate population statistics for the African elephant, significantly increasing the reported number so as to make it appear

that the largest terrestrial mammal was not on the verge of becoming an endangered species.

3 This reading of the *Phaedo* draws from and is indebted to the work of John Sallis (1987: 1).

Chapter 3 In Medias Res

1 Another example from *Fawlty Towers* that illustrates the difference between *Vorhandenheit* and *Zuhandenheit* can be seen during the opening credits of each episode when the name of the hotel that gives the programme its title is seen on a signpost rearranged each week in a different fashion to form comical and even obscene alternative spellings.

2 Also philosophically determined to confront things in all their stubborn thingness, for his part, Jean-Paul Sartre supplemented his existential classic *Being and Nothingness* with explicitly literary explorations of its phenomenological concepts. Thus, in *Nausea*, the protagonist Roquentin is momentarily overwhelmed by the implacable treeness of the chestnut tree he is sitting opposite in a Parisian park and describes the experience in terms that would not be out of place in either his or Heidegger's philosophical tracts:

> That root, with its colour, its shape, its frozen movement, was ... beneath all explanation. Each of its qualities escaped from it a little, flowed out of it, half-solidified, almost became a thing; each one was *superfluous in* the root, and the whole stump now gave me the impression of rolling a little outside itself, denying itself, losing itself in a strange excess. I scraped my heel against that black claw: I should have liked to peel off a little of the bark. For no particular reason, out of defiance, to make the absurd pink of an abrasion appear on the tanned leather: to *play* with the absurdity of the world. But when I took

my foot away, I saw that the bark was still black ... It *resembled* a colour but also ... a bruise or again a secretion, a yoke – and something else, a smell for example, it melted into a smell of wet earth, of warm, moist wood, into a black smell spread like varnish over that sinewy wood, into a taste of sweet, pulped fibre. I didn't *see* that black in a simple way: sight is an abstract invention, a cleaned-up simplified idea, a human idea. That black, a weak, amorphous presence, far surpassed sight, smell, and taste. But that richness became confusion and finally ceased to be anything at all because it was too much. (Sartre 1983 [1938]: 186–7)

Chapter 4 Media Apps: The Questions Concerning Technology

1 For individuals who have grown up in the digital era, amateur radio is probably a foreign or forgotten aspect of twentieth-century culture. In its time (beginning in the 1930s and gaining considerable popularity after the Second World War), 'ham radio', as it was called, was the internet of its age, allowing amateur radio operators to connect to and interact with individuals all over the globe by leveraging the technological capabilities of radio. Ham radio enthusiasts not only operated the equipment but often built their own sets from kits and army surplus electronics. This do-it-yourself (DIY) approach to information technology continued in the PC-era with the Home Brew Computer Club of Silicon Valley and the efforts of DIY inventors like Steve Jobs and Steve Wozniak, who assembled the first Apple computer in a garage.

2 *Ratio* is the term Kracauer uses to express the concept of instrumental reason and its various manifestations in the culture industry. It is, as Heidegger points out on a number of occasions, one of the standard translations of *logos* and

one of the reasons that in *Being and Time* he deploys the
term *Rede* to name not the instrumental aspects of language but its originary dimension. It is crucial differences
like this that complicate efforts to relate Heidegger's work
to other theorists and that require careful attention to his
texts and language.

3 Interestingly, *Dasein*, as the term was used in *Being and
   Time*, does not appear in the text of QCT. This is consistent with the fact that Heidegger, since *the turn*, turns away
   from the analysis of *Dasein* that had characterized his early
   efforts. For this reason, the neologism *Dasign* functions as
   the trace of erasure (Derrida 1982 [1972]: 24) – the mark
   left by the absence of a mark.

REFERENCES

Works by Heidegger

AWP Heidegger, M. 1977 [1952]. 'The Age of the World Picture'. Trans. William Lovitt. In *The Question Concerning Technology and Other Essays*. New York: Harper Torchbooks, pp. 115–54. *Die Zeit des Weltbildes* in *Holzwege*. Frankfurt am Main: Vittorio Klostermann.

BAT Heidegger, M. 2010 [2001]. *Being and Truth*. Trans. G. Fried and R. Polt. Bloomington, IN: Indiana University Press. *Sein und Wahrheit*. Frankfurt am Main: Vittorio Klostermann.

BDT Heidegger, M. 1971 [1954]. 'Building Dwelling Thinking'. Trans. Albert Hofstadter. In *Poetry, Language, Thought*. New York: Harper and Row, pp. 143–62. *Vorträge und Aufsätze*. Pfullingen: Verlag Günther Neske, pp. 139–56.

BFL Heidegger, M. 2012 [1994]. *Bremen and Freiburg Lectures: Insight into That Which Is and The Basic*

Principles of Thinking. Trans. Andrew J. Mitchell. Bloomington, IN: Indiana University Press. *Bremer und Freiburger Vorträge.* Frankfurt am Main: Vittorio Klostermann.

BPP   Heidegger, M. 1982 [1975]. *Basic Problems of Phenomenology.* Trans. Albert Hofstadter. Bloomington, IN: Indiana University Press. *Die Grundprobleme der Phänomenologie.* Frankfurt am Main: Vittorio Klostermann.

BQP   Heidegger, M. 1994 [1984]. *Basic Questions of Philosophy: Selected 'Problems' of 'Logic'.* Trans. R. Rojcewicz and A. Schuwer. Bloomington: Indiana University Press. *Grundfragen der Philosophie: Ausgewählte 'Probleme' der 'Logik'.* Frankfurt am Main: Vittorio Klostermann.

BT   Heidegger, M. 1962 [1984]. *Being and Time.* Trans. J. Macquarrie and E. Robinson. New York: Harper and Row. *Sein und Zeit.* Tübingen: Max Niemeyer Verlag.

CTP   Heidegger, M. 2012 [1989]. *Contributions to Philosophy (of the Event).* Trans. Richard Rojcewicz and Daniela Vallega-Neu. Bloomington, IN: Indiana University Press. *Beiträge zur Philosophie (Vom Ereignis).* Frankfurt am Main: Vittorio Klostermann.

DOT   Heidegger, M. 1966 [1959]. *Discourse on Thinking.* Trans. J. M. Anderson and E. H. Freund. New York: Harper & Row. *Gelassenheit.* Pfullingen: Verlag Günther Neske.

EGT   Heidegger, M. 1975 [1954]. *Early Greek Thinking.* Trans. David Farrell Krell and Frank Capuzzi. New York: Harper and Row. *Vorträge und Aufsätze.* Pfullingen: Verlag Günther Neske.

EOP   Heidegger, M. 1972 [1969]. 'The End of Philosophy and the Task of Thinking'. Trans. Joan Stambaugh.

In *On Time and Being*. New York: Harper Torchbooks. *Zur Sache des Denkens*. Tübingen: Max Niemeyer Verlag.

ITM Heidegger, M. 2000 [1953]. *Introduction to Metaphysics*. Trans. Gregory Fried and Richard Polt. New Haven, CT: Yale University Press. *Einführung in die Metaphysik*. Tübingen: Max Niemeyer Verlag.

LAN Heidegger, Martin. 1971 [1959]. 'Language'. In *Poetry, Language, Thought*. Trans. Albert Hofstadter, New York: Harper and Row, pp. 189–210. *Unterwegs zur Sprache*. Pfullingen: Verlag Günther Neske.

LET Heidegger, M. 2009 [1998]. *Logic as the Question Concerning the Essence of Language*. Trans. Wanda Torres Gregory and Yvonne Una. Albany, NY: State University of New York Press. *Logik als die Frage nach dem Wesen der Sprache*. Frankfurt am Main: Vittorio Klosterman.

LOH Heidegger, M. 1977 [1967]. 'The Letter on Humanism'. Trans. F. A. Capuzzi. In D. Krell (ed.), *Martin Heidegger Basic Writings*. New York: Harper and Row, pp. 189–242. *Wegmarken*. Frankfurt am Main: Vittorio Klostermann.

LQT Heidegger, M. 2010 [1976]. *Logic: The Question of Truth*. Trans. Thomas Sheehan. Bloomington, IN: Indiana University Press. *Logik: Die Frage nach der Wahrheit*. Frankfurt am Main: Vittorio Klostermann.

NOL Heidegger, M. 1971 [1959]. 'The Nature of Language.' In *On the Way to Language*. Trans. Peter D. Hertz. New York: Harper and Row, pp. 57–111. *Unterwegs zur Sprache*. Pfullingen: Verlag Günther Neske.

OEL Heidegger, M. 2004 [1999]. *On the Essence of Language. The Metaphysics of Language and the Essencing of the Word. Concerning Herder's Treatise on the Origin of Language*. Trans. Wanda Torres Gregory and Yvonne Unna. Albany, NY: State University of New York Press. *Vom Wesen der Sprache. Die Metaphysik der Sprache und die Wesung des Wortes. Zu Herders Abhandlung Über den Ursprung der Sprache*. Frankfurt am Main: Vittorio Klostermann.

OET Heidegger, M. 1977 [1967]. 'On the Essence of Truth'. Trans. J. Sallis. In D. Krell (ed.), *Martin Heidegger Basic Writings*. New York: Harper and Row, pp. 117–41. *Wegmarken*. Frankfurt am Main: Vittorio Klostermann.

OGS Heidegger, M. 2010 [1976]. 'Only a God Can Save Us: *Der Spiegel* Interview'. Trans. William J. Richardson. In Thomas Sheehan (ed.), *Heidegger: The Man and the Thinker*. New Brunswick, NJ: Transaction Publishers, pp. 45–68.

OWA Heidegger, M. 1971 [1960]. 'The Origin of the Work of Art'. Trans. Albert Hofstadter. In *Poetry, Language, Thought*. New York: Harper and Row, pp. 17–87. *Der Ursprung des Kunstwerkes*. Stuttgart: Reclam.

PDT Heidegger, M. 1998 [1967]. 'Plato's Doctrine of Truth'. Trans. T. Sheehan. In W. McNeill (ed.), *Pathmarks*. Cambridge: Cambridge University Press, pp. 155–82. *Wegmarken*. Frankfurt am Main: Vittorio Klostermann.

PMD Heidegger, M. 1971 [1954]. '. . . Poetically Man Dwells . . .' Trans. Albert Hofstadter. In *Poetry, Language, Thought*. New York: Harper and Row, pp. 213–29. *Vorträge und Aufsätze*. Pfullingen: Verlag Günther Neske, pp. 181–98.

QCT Heidegger, M. 1977 [1962]. 'The Question Concerning Technology'. Trans. William Lovitt. In *The Question Concerning Technology and Other Essays*. New York: Harper Torchbooks, pp. 3–35. *Die*

Frage nach der Technik in *Die Technik und die Kehre*. Pfullingen: Verlag Günther Neske.

TL Heidegger, M. 1998 [1962]. 'Traditional Language and Technological Language'. Trans. Wanda Torres Gregory. *Journal of Philosophical Inquiry* 23(2): 129–45.

TT Heidegger, M. 1971 [1954]. 'The Thing'. Trans. Albert Hofstadter. In *Poetry, Language, Thought*. New York: Harper and Row, pp. 165–82. *Vorträge und Aufsätze*, pp. 157–180. Pfullingen: Verlag Günther Neske.

TUR Heidegger, M. 1977 [1962]. 'The Turning'. Trans. William Lovitt. In *The Question Concerning Technology and Other Essays*. New York: Harper Torchbooks, pp. 36–52. *'Die Kehre'*. In *Die Technik und die Kehre*. Pfullingen: Verlag Günther Neske.

WCT Heidegger, M. 1968 [1954]. *What is Called Thinking?* Trans. J. Glenn Gray. New York: Harper Torchbook. *Was Heisst Denken?* Tübingen: Max Niemeyer Verlag.

WIT Heidegger, M. 1967 [1962]. *What is a Thing?* Trans. W. B. Barton and Vera Deutsch. Chicago: Henry Regnery Company. *Die Frage nach dem Ding*. Tübingen: Max Niemeyer Verlag.

WTL Heidegger, Martin. 1993 [1959]. 'The Way to Language'. In *Martin Heidegger: Basic Writings*, 2nd edn. Trans. and ed. David Farrell Krell. San Francisco, CA: Harper Collins, pp. 393–426. *Unterwegs zur Sprache*. Pfullingen: Verlag Günther Neske.

Other works

Adilkno. 1998. *Media Archive*. New York: Autonomedia.

Adorno, T. W. 1991. *The Culture Industry: Selected Essays on Mass Culture*, ed. J. M. Bernstein. London: Routledge.

Adorno, T. W. 1991 [1938]. 'Fetish Character in Music and the Regression of Listening', in J. M. Bernstein (ed.), *The Culture Industry: Selected Essays on Mass Culture*. New York: Routledge. Originally published in *Zeitschrift für Sozialforschung*, vol. VII, Paris: Alcan.

Adorno, T. W. 1997. *Aesthetic Theory*, ed. Gretel Adorno and Rolf Tiedemann, trans. Robert Hullot-Kentor. Minneapolis: University of Minnesota Press.

Allen, W. 1977. *Annie Hall*. Hollywood, CA: United Artists.

Andrejevic, M. 2009. 'Critical Media Studies 2.0: An Interactive Upgrade'. *Interactions: Studies in Communication and Culture* 1(1): 35–51.

Arendt, H. 19 . *Eichmann in Jersualem: A Report on the Banality of Evil*. New York: Penguin Books.

Barthes, R. 1973 [1957] *Mythologies*. London: Paladin Books.

Baudrillard, J. 1984 [1981]. *Simulations*, trans. Paul Foss, Paul Patton and Philip Beitchman. New York: Semiotext(e). *Simulacres et Simulation*. Paris: Editions Galilée.

Baudrillard, J. 1983 [1978]. *In the Shadow of the Silent Majorities*, trans. P. Foss et al. New York: Semiotext(e). *A L'Ombre des majorités ou la fin du social*. Paris: Cahier Quatre d'Utopie.

Baudrillard. J. 1988 [1987]. *The Ecstasy of Communication*. New York: Semiotext(e). Paris: Editions Grasset.

Baudrillard, J. 1990 [1979]. *Seduction*. New York: St. Martin's Press. *De la séduction*. Paris: Editions Galilée.

Baudrillard, J. 2002 [1995]. *The Perfect Crime*, trans. Chris Turner. New York: Verso. *Le crime parfait*. Editions Galilée.

Baudrillard, J. 2005 [2004]. 'The Intelligence of Evil, or the Lucidity Pact', trans. Chris Turner. Oxford: Berg. *Le Pacte de lucidité ou l'intelligence du Mal*. Paris: Editions Galilée.

Bauman, Z. 1989. *Modernity and the Holocaust*. Cambridge: Polity Press.

Bennington, G. and Derrida, J. 1993 [1991]. *Jacques Derrida*, trans. Geoffrey Bennington. Chicago: University of Chicago Press. *Jacques Derrida*. Paris: Editions du Seuil.

Benjamin, W. 1969. *Illuminations*, trans. Harry Zohn. New York: Schocken Books.

Benjamin, W. 1973 [1936]. 'The Work of Art in the Age of Mechanical Reproduction', trans. H. Zohn. In *Illuminations*. New York: Schocken, pp. 217–52.

Benso, S. 2000. *The Face of Things: A Different Side of Ethics*. Albany, NY: State University of New York Press.

Berger, P. and Luckmann, T. 1966. *The Social Construction of Reality*. New York: Anchor Books.

Bernet, R. 1994. 'Phenomenological Reduction and the Double Life of the Subject', in Theodore J. Kiesl and John Van Buren (eds), *Reading Heidegger from the Start: Essays in His Earliest Thought*. Albany, NY: State University of New York Press, pp. 245–68.

Bernstein, R. J. 1996. *Hannah Arendt and the Jewish Question*. Cambridge, MA: MIT Press.

Bolter, J. D. 1991. *Writing Space: The Computer, Hypertext, and the History of Writing*. Hillsdale, NJ: Lawrence Erlbaum Associates.

Bolter, J. D. and Grusin, R. 2000. *Remediation: Understanding New Media*. Cambridge, MA: MIT Press.

Carey, J. 1989. *Communication as Culture: Essays on Media and Society*. New York: Routledge.

Chandler, D. 1996. 'Shaped and Being Shaped: Engaging with Media'. *Computer-Mediated Communication Magazine*, 1 February. www.december.com/cmc/mag/1996/feb/chandler.html, last accessed 27 November 2013.

Chang, B. 1996. *Deconstructing Communication: Representation, Subject and Economies of Exchange*. Minneapolis, MN: University of Minnesota Press.

Comedy Central. 2006. 'The Colbert Report'. Video Clips available at http://comedycentral.com.

Cooley, C. H. 1962. *Social Organization*. New York: Schocken Books.

Dallmayr, F. R. 1989. 'Adorno and Heidegger'. *Diacritics* 19(3–4): 82–100.

Davidson, A. 1989. 'Questions concerning Heidegger: Opening the Debate'. *Critical Inquiry* 15(2) (Winter): 407–26.

de Beistegui, M. 2005. *The New Heidegger*. New York: Continuum.

Debord, G. 1970 [1967]. *The Society of the Spectacle*, trans. F. Perlman and J. Supak. Detroit, MI: Black and Red. *La Société du spectacle*. Paris: Buchet-Chastel.

Dennett, Daniel C. 1996. *Kinds of Minds: Toward an Understanding of Consciousness*. New York: Basic Books.

Derrida, D. 1976 [1967]. *Of Grammatology*, trans. Gayatri Chakravorty Spivak. Baltimore, MD: Johns Hopkins University Press. *De la Grammatologie*. Paris: Les Editions de Minuit.

Derrida, J. 1981 [1972]. *Positions*, trans. Alan Bass. Chicago: University of Chicago Press. *Positions*, Les Editions de Minuit.

Derrida, D. 1982 [1972]. *Margins of Philosophy*, trans. Alan Bass. Chicago: University of Chicago Press. *Marges de la philosophie*. Paris: Les Editions de Minuit.

Derrida, J. 1988. *Limited Inc*, trans. by Samuel Weber. Evanston, IL: Northwestern University Press.

Derrida, D. 1991. 'Letter to a Japanese Friend', in P. Kamuf (ed.), *A Derrida Reader: Between the Blinds*, New York: Columbia University Press, pp. 270–6.

Derrida, D. 1993. Afterword to *Limited Inc.*, trans. Samuel Weber. Evanston, IL: Northwestern University Press, pp. 111–54.

Descartes, R. 1988 [1983]. *The Philosophical Writings of Descartes*, vol. 1, trans. J. Cottingham, R. Stoothoff and D. Murdoch. Cambridge: Cambridge University Press. *Oeuvres de Descartes* in 11 vols. C. Adam and P. Tannery (eds). Paris: Librairie Philosophique.

Descartes, R. 1991 [1983]. *The Philosophical Writings of Descartes*, vol. 3, trans. J. Cottingham, R. Stoothoff, D. Murdoch and A. Kenny. Cambridge: Cambridge University Press. *Oeuvres de Descartes* in 11 vols. C. Adam and P. Tannery (eds). Paris: Librairie Philosophique.

Dourish, P. 2004. *Where the Action Is: The Foundations of Embodied Interaction*. Cambridge, MA: MIT Press.

Durkheim, E. 2008 [1912]. *Elementary Forms of Religious Life*. Oxford: Oxford Classics.

Dwan, D. 2003. 'Idle Talk: Ontology and Mass Communication in Heidegger'. *New Formations* 51: 113–27.

Eagleton, T. 2003. *Literary Theory: An Introduction*. Minneapolis, MN: University of Minnesota Press.

Edwards, P. 2004. *Heidegger's Confusions*. Amherst, NY: Prometheus Books.

Ellul, J. 1964 [1954]. *The Technological Society*, trans. John Wilkinson. New York: Vintage. *La Technique ou l'enjeu du siècle*. Paris: Librairie Armand Colin.

Feenberg, A. 1999. *Questioning Technology*. New York: Routledge.

Fry, T. 1993. *RIUIAITV? Heidegger and the Televisual*. Sydney: Power Publications.

Gasche, R. 1986. *The Tain of the Mirror: Derrida and the Philosophy of Reflection*. Cambridge, MA: Harvard University Press.

Gregory, W. T. 2007. 'Unintelligibility in Heidegger'. *The Proceedings of the Twenty-First World Congress of Philosophy*, vol. 11, pp. 57–61.

Guignon, C. B. 1983. *Heidegger and the Problem of Knowledge*. Indianapolis, IN: Hackett.

Gunkel, D. 2011. 'To Tell the Truth: The Internet and Emergent Epistemological Challenges in Social Research', in Sharlene Hesse-Biber (ed.), *The Handbook of Emergent Technologies in Social Research*. New York: Oxford University Press, pp. 47–64.

Harman, G. 2002. *Tool Being: Heidegger and the Metaphysics of Objects*. Peru, IL: Open Court Publishing.

Harman, G. 2010. 'Technology, objects and things in Heidegger'. *Cambridge Journal of Economics* 34(1): 17–25. First published online 29 May 2009.

Hayles, N. K. 1999. *How We Became Posthuman: Virtual Bodies in Cybernetics, Literature and Informatics*. Chicago: University of Chicago Press.

Heim, M. 1993. *The Metaphysics of Virtual Reality*. New York: Oxford University Press.

Husserl, E. 1975 [1970]. *Logical Investigations*, trans. J. N. Findlay. New Jersey: Humanities Press International. *Logische Untersuchungen*. Tübingen: Max Niemeyer Verlag.

Innis, H. 1951. *The Bias of Communication*. Toronto: University of Toronto Press.

Jameson, F. (ed.) 1980. *Aesthetics and Politics*. London: Verso.

Jones, B. 1990. *Sleepers, Wake! Technology and the Future of Work*. New York: Oxford University Press.

Kant, I. 1965 [1956]. *Critique of Pure Reason*, trans. Norman Kemp Smith. New York: St. Martin's Press. *Kritik der reinen Vernunft*. Hamburg: Felix Meiner Verlag.

Kittler, F. A. 1999 [1986]. *Gramophone, Film, Typewriter*, trans. G. Winthrop-Young and M. Wutz. Stanford, CA: Stanford University Press. *Grammophon, Film, Typewriter*. Berlin: Brinkmann and Bose.

Kracauer, S. 1995 [1963]. *The Mass Ornament: Weimar Essays*, trans. Thomas Y. Levin. Cambridge, MA: Harvard

University Press. *Das Ornament der Masse: Essays*. Frankfurt am Main: Suhrkamp Verlag.

Lafont, C. 2000 [1994]. *Heidegger, Language and World-Disclosure*, trans. Graham Harman. Cambridge: Cambridge University Press. *Sprache und Welterschliessung*. Frankfurt am Main: Suhrkamp Verlag.

Lévy, P. 2001 [1997]. *Cyberculture*, trans. Robert Bononno. Minneapolis, MN: University of Minnesota Press. *Cyberculture*. Paris: Éditions Odile Jacob/Éditions du Conseil de l'Europe.

Lucena, A. D. 2009. 'Thinking About Technology, But . . . In Ortega's or in Heidegger's Style?' *Argumentos de Razón Técnica* 12(1): 99–123.

Marcuse, H. 2002 [1964]. *One-Dimensional Man*. Boston, MA: Beacon Books.

Maturana, H. R. and Varela, F. J. 1980. *Autopoiesis and Cognition: The Realization of the Living*. Dordrecht: D. Reidel.

McLuhan, M. 1962. *The Gutenberg Galaxy: The Making of Typographical Man*. Toronto: University of Toronto Press.

McLuhan, M. 1995. *Understanding Media: The Extensions of Man*. Cambridge, MA: MIT Press.

McLuhan, M. 1997. 'Notes on Burroughs', in M. Moos (ed.), *Media Research: Technology, Art, Communication*. Amsterdam: Overseas Publishers Association.

Nakamura, L. 2007. *Digitizing Race: Visual Cultures of the Internet*. Minneapolis, MN: University of Minnesota Press.

Plato. 1982. *Phaedrus*, trans. Harold North Fowler. Cambridge, MA: Harvard University Press.

Plato. 1987. *Republic*, trans. Paul Shorey. Cambridge, MA: Harvard University Press.

Plato 1990. *Phaedo*, trans. H. N. Fowler. Cambridge, MA: Harvard University Press.

Poster, M. 1995. *The Second Media Age*. Cambridge: Polity Press.

Postman, N. 2000. *Building a Bridge to the 18th Century*. New York: Vintage Books.

Richardson, W. J. 2003. *Heidegger: Through Phenomenology to Thought*. New York: Fordham University Press.

Ronell, A. 1989. *The Telephone Book: Technology, Schizophrenia, Electric Speech*. Lincoln, NB: University of Nebraska Press.

Rosenberg, B. and White, D. M. 1957. *Mass Culture: The Popular Arts in America*. Toronto: Collier-MacMillan.

Rötzer, F. 1998. *Digitale Weltentwürfe: Streifzüge Durch die Netzkultur*. Wien: Karl Hanser Verlag.

Rüdiger, F. 2004. 'The Mathematical and the Metaphysical Roots of Modern Technological Thought: Reading Heidegger'. *Revista FAMECOS* 24: 73–83.

Rüdiger, F. 2006. *Martin Heidegger e a Questão da Técnica*. Porto Alegra, Brazil: Editora Sulina.

Ruin, H. 2005. 'Contributions to Philosophy', in Hubert L. Dreyfus and Mark A. Wrathall (eds), *A Companion to Heidegger*. Oxford: Blackwell, pp. 358–74.

Sallis, J. 1987. *Spacings – of Reason and Imagination in the Texts of Kant, Fichte, Hegel*. Chicago: University of Chicago Press.

Sapir, E. 1941 [1929]. 'The Status of Linguistics as a Science', in David G. Mandelbaum (ed.), *Selected Writings of Edward Sapir in Language, Culture and Personality*. Berkeley, CA: University of California Press, pp. 160–6.

Sartre, J.-P. 1983 [1938]. *Nausea*. London: Penguin.

Scannell, P. 1996. *Radio, Television and Modern Life*. Oxford: Blackwell.

Scott, J. M. 2005. 'Fancy Her Femme. Flirting with an OPEN Sexual Aesthetic', in Lisa N. Gurley, Claudia Leeb and Anna Aloisia Moser (eds), *Feminists Contest Politics and Philosophy*. Brussels: Peter Lang, pp. 35–44.

Searle, J. 2000. 'The Limits of Phenomenology', in M. Wrathall and J. Malpas (eds), *Heidegger, Coping, and Cognitive Science: Essays in Honor of Hubert L. Dreyfus*, vol. 2. Cambridge, MA: MIT Press.

Shannon, C. E. and Weaver, W. 1963. *The Mathematical Theory of Communication*. Urbana, IL: University of Illinois Press.

Sheehan, T. 2001. 'A Paradigm Shift in Heidegger Research'. *Continental Philosophy Review* 32(2): 1–20.

Sloterdijk, P. 1987 [1983]. *Critique of Cynical Reason*, trans. Michael Eldred. Minneapolis, MN: University of Minnesota Press. *Kritik der Zynischen Vernunft*. Frankfurt am Main: Suhrkamp Verlag.

Sontag, S. 1979. *On Photography*. London: Penguin.

Sterne, J. 2005. *The Audible Past: Cultural Origins of Sound Reproduction*. Durham, NC: Duke University Press.

Stiegler, B. 2009 [1996]. *Technics and Time v.2: Disorientation*, trans. Stephen Barker. Stanford, CA: Stanford University Press. *La Technique et le temps 2. La Désorientation*. Editions Galilée.

Taylor, P. A. and Harris, J. Ll. 2008. *Critical Theories of Mass Media: Then and Now*. Maidenhead: McGraw Hill.

Thoreau, H. D. 1910. *Walden*. New York: Thomas Y. Crowell & Company.

Virilio, P. 1997 [1995]. *Open Sky*, trans. Julie Rose. New York: Verso. *La Vitesse de Libération*. Paris: Editions Galilée.

Wiener, N. 1950. *The Human Use of Human Beings: Cybernetics and Society*. New York: Da Capo Press.

Wiener, N. 1961. *Cybernetics: Or Control and Communication in the Animal and the Machine*. Cambridge, MA: MIT Press.

Winner, L. 1977. *Autonomous Technology: Technics-out-of-*

Control as a Theme in Political Thought. Cambridge, MA: MIT Press.

Wittgenstein, L. 1995 [1922]. *Tractatus Logico-Philosophicus*. New York: Routledge.

Wolf, G. 1996. 'Channeling McLuhan'. *Wired* 4(1). www.wired.com/wired/archive/4.01/channeling_pr.html, last accessed 27 November 2013.

Wrathall, M. A. 2011. *Heidegger and Unconcealment: Truth, Language, and History*. Cambridge: Cambridge University Press.

Zimmerman, M. E. 1990. *Heidegger's Confrontation with Modernity: Technology, Politics, Art*. Bloomington, IN: Indiana University Press.

Žižek, S. 1991. *For They Know Not What They Do: Enjoyment as a Political Factor*. New York: Verso.

Žižek, S. 2006a. 'Philosophy, the "Unknown Knowns", and the Public Use of Reason'. *Topoi* 25(1–2): 137–42.

Žižek, S. 2006b. *The Parallax View*. Cambridge, MA: MIT Press.

Žižek, S. 2008. *Violence*. New York: Picador.

Ziolkowski, T. 2001. 'Five Portraits: Modernity and the Imagination in Twentieth-Century German Writing' (Review). *Modernism/modernity* 8(2): 359–60.

INDEX